Creating
Discovery
Journals

Karen Skidmore Rackliffe

First Printing: May 1999
Second Printing: March 2000
Third Printing: August 2000
Fourth Printing: November 2001

Published by: Karen Skidmore Rackliffe
                 Salt Lake City, Utah
  email: WildDays@Rackliffe.org

Production by: www.SunriseBooks.com

Library of Congress Card Number: 99-63950
ISBN: 1-57636-073-3

TABLE OF CONTENTS

For ye shall go out with joy,
and be led forth with peace:
the mountains and
the hills shall break
forth before you into singing,
and all the trees of the field
shall clap their hands.

—Isaiah 55:12

March 7th 1996
Murray Park & Enoch

Introduction: Wild Days

S ome days are wild days with ringing phones, buzzing doorbells, beeping microwaves, pagers and clocks. There are mounds of laundry and dishes and junk mail and bills to sort and process. There are places to be, appointments to keep, a list of things to do that lengthens twice for every item crossed off. Most of it has no meaning. It is the backlash of our efficient, industrialized society, where we try to do everything, all the time, every day. Picking up the dry cleaning, rotating the tires on the car, returning the weekend videos. Yes, the logical mind argues, "It must be done." But how and when do we recharge our symbolic batteries and fill the empty recesses of our own hearts? These many details crowd out time for our own souls. We need time away from our hectic lives to live, to connect with ourselves, our world, our creator and one another. Where in our planners do we fit the nourishing expansive delights of writing down our thoughts about life, watching a spider build his web, praying, or looking into the eyes of a child to find who lives there?

When I was eleven, my mother took me to a doctor for my ailments. He gave me a diagnosis: mononucleosis and stress. He looked over the top of his bifocals and told me to stay home from school and rest completely. Then my mother took me to an artist friend of hers who gave me more advice. I remember her kindly wrinkled face, and her eyes when she said, "Promise me that you will spend time every day watching the clouds. Watch them move and spin. Look for animals hidden in their curls. Look for castles and dream. Dream. You can find your dreams in the clouds." I believed them both. I stayed home from school half of the sixth grade. I took my medicine. I looked at clouds. (And when my mother wasn't watching I read everything I could slip from the bookshelves.) My sixth grade teacher came to visit me once at the end of the term. We talked for a time. I showed him a report on Australia I had put together from a National Geographic magazine. He told my mother I didn't have to do any more school work. I had advanced past my classmates and would be ready for junior high. I must have learned a lot from the clouds out my window.

But, that was then, and, now is now. I am a *grownup* with responsibilities. I am a wife, a mother of seven, a daughter, a church member, a friend, a volunteer, a teacher, a housekeeper, and so on. I am so many things that I begin to lose who I am. Lists suck away at my soul. Yet, the lists become longer. I rush about frantically, like a wild thing, trapped. But the trap is of my own making. I want to be all of those things. I just need a little space to remember why I have chosen them. I need a window and a breath of sea air. I need a door to go out, so I can come back in again.

So, when days are wild, I grab a journal and pen and head out the door. I leave behind the phones and buzzers, beeps and lists. I tell my children and parents, friends or husband, "I'm going crazy. You come too." So, we go to some wild place to watch the clouds, the river, the birds, the blossoms, the wildlife. It's like coming home. Home to the planet where I was born and where I grow. A place where my body can rest while my spirit soars. I have with me my loved ones, my thoughts, an open heart for discovery and my journal to record my wild days. I bring my journal to capture these golden wild moments: the sudden stillness of a deer watching, the smell of rain in the pines, the songs of hidden birds, the bigger children helping the smaller ones to cross a stream, the taste of sun-filled wild blackberries. I record these in my journal in words and pictures. They will feed me on darker days.

Every blade of grass
has its angel
that bends over it
and whispers,
"Grow, grow."

—Talmud

Chapter 1

INTRODUCING DISCOVERY JOURNALS TO KIDS

When I first introduced discovery journals to my children I called them Wild Days. After a particularly exasperating week I gathered my children into the family room and said;

"I am tired of the phones, and the chores, the work and the school stuff. Today is a Wild Day. I am going to do something Wild. You can stay here or you can come with me, but you better have shoes and a canteen."

My children all ran for their socks and shoes. They leapt at the opportunity to escape routine cares. They asked a million questions which I dodged and parried as they piled into the van. We picked up Grandma and Grandpa, who are always game for an adventure with the grandkids. We drove about thirty minutes to a nearby canyon, stopping by a spring river in full flood. We examined the banks for erosion and flood trauma. We spotted birds and mammals. The new spring growth had just begun to bud forth. The children explored. My mother and I got out our paints and started playing with the colors. She studied a pine cone while I recorded the strata of colors on the bare cliff face. After a relaxing amount of time had passed, I got out the bag of cookies I had so cleverly concealed in the backpack of art supplies. The children sensed its presence immediately, gathering around the picnic table.

"What are the cookies for, Mom?"

"Oh, these? They are for artistic inspiration."

"What?"

"For people who paint in the canyon."

"Mom? Can I paint too?"

"You bet."

I handed them their new discovery journals.

"Artists need to have real art journals," I explained. "Find something interesting here in the canyon to paint with words or colors."

They all chose watercolors. They all got a cookie.

"Now put the date on the page."

They all got another cookie.

"Can you write a little about the day?"

They all got another cookie.

"Would you like to do this again sometime?"

"Sure, how 'bout tomorrow!"

We finished the cookies and went home.

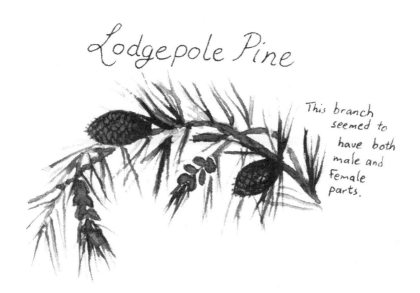

Lodgepole Pine

This branch seemed to have both male and female parts.

Chapter 2

DISCOVERY JOURNALS

I began keeping diaries as a child. My grandmother gave me a little lined book with a key for my eighth birthday. It was fun for a while. But, the blank pages made me feel guilty and the four tiny lines a day never seemed adequate for what I had to say. In Junior High I switched to spiral bound notebooks. They had plenty of lines. I could date them as I wrote. I regretted losing the lock, but they looked just like school work so no one bothered looking at them. I could even write in class undisturbed. When I was fifteen, my sister gave me a blank book. I experimented with pictures and poems on its liberating white pages. College expanded my thoughts. Science notes merged with poems and current events. Marginal doodlings decorated my thoughts.

When my children came along, it was all I could manage to keep their baby books informed of their milestones. Their milestones of crawling and walking became my miles too. Now I journey with my children. We journal together too. Discovery journals have opened up a new way of looking at the world for me and my children. I have discovered that when you travel with a child there are adventures in every leaf and bud.

There are many kinds of journals, as there are many journeys in life. A journal is a record kept while you travel. Nature notebooks generally refer to a journal dedicated to observations of the natural world. Diaries record daily events. Sketch books are used by artists to record visual impressions.

Lab notes or field notes imply serious scientific study and observation.

Journals are a place to remember thoughts, ideas, images, dreams, events, developments, musings and hopes. Discoveries are flashes of thought that make the world seem somehow brighter, more beautiful, interesting, or bizarre.

A discovery journal places moments of insights together, page upon page, building connections between seasons and years. It is a record of days, a bringing together of scattered experience into a meaningful whole.

A discovery journal can be a wonderful teaching tool for the individual. It is our interpretation of our own experience. By using the skills of writing, drawing, observing, analyzing, imagining, graphing, and recording we expand our understanding of the world and ourselves. Likewise, these valuable skills can be taught to our children.

Discovery journals are great fun in the classroom. The long hours and daily grind of the classroom tend to wear on the students and the teacher. A Wild Day can be a great way to get the spark back in a science lesson, purpose in an art lesson, or creativity back into book reports. Journal discoveries often spark other interests that lead to more research. Because of its flexible nature, these journals are enjoyable for families as they encourage education in the home. It can be a life long learning tool for all.

So, what is a discovery journal? A sketch book? A diary? A nature notebook? An account book? Lab notes? Musings? A field journal? Rantings? A record book? Letters unsent? A discovery journal can be all of these. It is a book you write yourself about anything that has importance to you. You make all the rules, and you can change them anyway you want.

There are many names for these personal books. I like the word journal because it implies a journey, a beginning and a

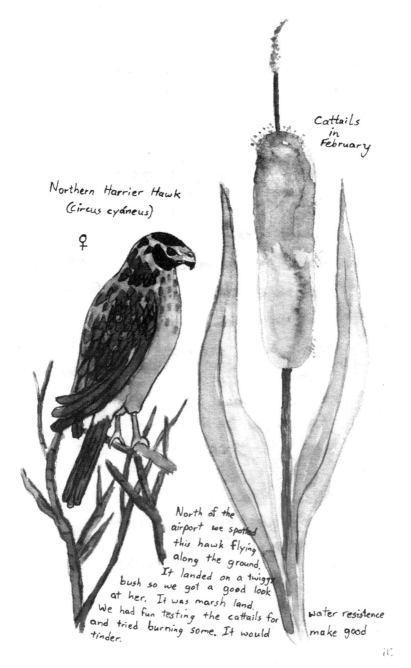

Cattails
in
February

Northern Harrier Hawk
(Circus cyáneus)

♀

North of the
airport we spotted
this hawk flying
along the ground.
It landed on a twiggy
bush so we got a good look
at her. It was marsh land.
We had fun testing the cattails for
and tried burning some. It would
tinder.

water resistence
make good

5/ Feb 24 1997
Cattails grow in wet
places. The leaves are very
long. The Indians used
the cattails for diapers
and for tinder. The roots
of this particular
plant are thick and strong
so the plant won't
break.

destination, with turning points along the way. I like to imagine my life as a journey, finding my way one step at a time.

And the discovery? That can also describe our lives. They are a chain of discoveries about the world, human nature, my own identity, and personal growth. In its pages I discover my journeys. I include the small and large moments of life that I want to remember. Like beads on a necklace, the days string together into patterns I will recognize when I look at the whole: the births of babies, Christmas celebrations, walks in the park, thoughts on religion or politics, sorrows or disappointments, great joy. These are all part of my world. I record them as they arrive. My journal ties them together and integrates the divergent features of my life.

Others may prefer to separate their thoughts into categories. Right now, my thirteen-year-old, Anita, prefers to have a separate art journal which she shares with me, and a separate daily event journal which is private. My nine-year-old, Riley, has a discovery journal which includes writings, drawings, and watercolors on nature adventures. He also keeps a special event journal where he records birthdays, vacations, new teeth, etc. He divides them in his mind between observations about nature (his favorite) and all the other stuff. Isaac, who is eleven, includes all sorts of things in his journal: comments or pictures about books he has read, jokes, portraits of famous artists and illustrations about holidays.

When I look back through the pages of their journals, I discover more about my children. I can see their interests taking shape. I can see what is important to them. I discover how they look at the world, each with a unique perspective. When I look back through my own recorded days, I find that my discovery journal concentrates on outings with my family. They are so very important to me. It seems I have painted a lot of birds, too. And wild flowers. There is very little recorded about the house or the laundry or the bills. Even though I spend so much time on these things, they are not treasures of my heart.

So, why not you! Why not keep a record of your thoughts and endeavors? A diary of your days and nights? Notes on all manners of interesting things you encounter? Poems, stories, pictures, charts, research, musings, schedules, lists, dreams, and ideas? But, I'm just an accountant, a housewife, a ten-year-old, a teacher, a grandpa, a mother, you say. Yes! You are! Your insights are valuable! They are important to you, your family, other's like you and other's unlike you. Who can resist a peek into someone else's private mind?

Journals have been used throughout the ages of mankind to record the thoughts, ideas, and discoveries of human endeavor. They are first hand accounts of great minds at work. Pliny used a journal in ancient times to record his fanciful ideas on plants and animals. Aristotle wrote down his ideas on philosophy and science. David kept his songs of the spirit. Leonardo Da Vinci sketched out his scientific and artistic discoveries. Marco Polo kept a record of his travels, his discoveries of new cultures and inventions. Columbus wrote two journals. The optimistic ship's log, which he kept for the encouragement of the crew, and his private writings, wrestlings with doubt and faith in himself and God. Lewis and Clark kept journals of their explorations into the uncharted west: making maps, explanations of weather, soil, plants, food, hardships, rivers, and notes on various Indian tribes. Thomas Jefferson wrote journals on horticulture. Henry David Thoreau recorded his own discoveries about himself and his countryside in remarkable literary style.

Many artists keep detailed sketch books as a reference and springboard to more finished art. Sketching is good even if you don't think of yourself as an artist. It concentrates your attention on details that are easily missed when thinking in words. The most interesting journals use words *and* sketches to communicate thoughts and feelings.

In many eras, journals were popular pastimes as well as the foundation of serious scientific and artistic study. All the explorers and naturalists we remember kept journals and drawings of their field work. Drawings were often included to clarify a point or add information before the advent of snapshots. Journal notes were essential in documenting new found information.

In late summer the Obedience plant flowers. It grows 3-4 feet tall, trying to crowd out the roses on the front walk. The bees, many varieties, love its blossoms. At the first rain the stalks bend as the blossoms fill with water. After the stalks are bent horizontal, the blooms will make a right angle turn to try to reach straight to the sun, trying to be obedient even after it has fallen.

In Victorian times, much like our own, there was an upsurge of interest in the natural world. Observations about the natural world were considered appropriate subjects for school and personal journals. Young girls were taught to paint wild flowers in botanical detail as part of their essential education. Boys kept notes on plants, insects, and animals found in the fields while hunting, or camping. It was the era of realism, sometimes called the Naturalistic Period in art, science, and literature.

In England we find Wordsworth, Stevenson, Tennyson, Hardy, Kipling, Browning, Burroughs, and Conrad. It was the age of Darwin, a master in observation and note taking. On the educational front, Charlotte Mason, a British educator, told parent groups and teachers in her college to encourage their students to keep nature notebooks.

In America, the popular books of the day were Thoreau's *Walden* (1854), Whitman's *Leaves of Grass* (1855), Longfellow's *Hiawatha* (1855), Alcott's *Little Women* (1868), and everything by Mark Twain. However, most Americans owned very few books. America's woefully meager libraries forced the schools to depend a great deal upon walks in the woods for science and chores on the farm for training. This, nevertheless, adequately prepared the population for the industrial revolution.

By the turn of the century, the wilderness so romanticized by these writers was almost gone. The buffalo, that symbol of the west, had been virtually exterminated. A new group of conservationists rose up determined to save what they could of the natural world. Teddy Roosevelt is a good example of this development. As a boy, he kept nature notebooks of animals and wild things. He dreamed of becoming a famous naturalist. When he grew up, his ambitions turned to politics but

he never forgot his interest in adventure or nature or the wilderness. He pushed through legislation which resulted in the national parks system, a refuge for wild animals and citizens alike.

Thomas Moran journeyed to Yellowstone country in Wyoming to witness and paint the stunning vistas and geothermal wonders of that landscape. He sent a collection of paintings back to Washington D.C. The public favor toward national parks rose and Teddy Roosevelt moved on the crest of that feeling to create our first national park, Yellowstone. I saw Thomas Moran's sketch book displayed in the park museum in the summer of 1998. The light delicacy of his watercolor sketches next to his finished landscapes beautifully captured the spiritual/mystical qualities of the Yellowstone Canyon, Mammoth Springs and Old Faithful. I felt his kindred love for the land and deep respect for creation as I studied his interpretation of what I was seeing with my own eyes. I too wanted to remember those scenes and explore my feelings of awe.

Concurrently, we find John Muir wandering the Sierras, publishing his stunning photographs and heartfelt comments on conservation and wilderness. His writings and art have drawn thousands of people to wild places.

Ernest Thompson Seton began the Woodcraft organization for boys which was patterned after Indian lore and values. Meanwhile, Lord Baden Powell founded the more militant organization of the Boy Scouts of England. These men corresponded, blended their concepts, and created the Boy Scouts of America. Later, Seton organized the Campfire program, returning back to many of his original ideas. Seton was a naturalist, illustrator, artist, and writer. He used journals extensively to capture his visual and literary ideas fresh in the field. This field study gave authenticity to his lively finished paintings, books, and short stories. The public loved his stuff. He wrote graphically about his lifetime of journal keeping.

> When in Toronto in 1881, preparing for this, my Western life, Doctor William Brodie, the naturalist, to whom I owe much, said to me: 'Now, don't fail to keep a journal of your Western travels. You will be sorry if you omit this. And you will value it more each year.' I began this at once. It is before me now. The first entry is dated: *Toronto, Ont., Monday, 13 Nov., 1881.* Saw three robins over the White Bridge.
>
> I wonder if anyone else ever got so much pure and subtle joy out of a simple statement as I did out of those first few words of record. They mean so little to others; but I felt instinctively that it was the beginning of what I wished to do. It was the first step into a glorious kingdom.
>
> And I kept on doing it—still do so: and the *Journal of my Travels and Doings* is on my desk before me—fifty fat leather volumes, most of them over-fat, and still increasing.
>
> Scribbled in pencil, ink, water color, anything; smirched with the blood of victims sacrificed on the alter of the knowledge-hunger; burned with sparks of the campfire; greasy with handling by unwashed, hasty, eager hands; badly written; at times badly illustrated with hasty sketches—hasty, but meaningful. A bookseller would not give a dime for the lot, and I would not part with them for a double million. They represent more than anything else those sixty years of my life and thought, my strivings and my joy.
>
> Aspiring young naturalists come to me for advice from time to time; and I always give them the counsel that helped me: Keep a full and accurate journal: and remember always, Science is measurement. (*The Worlds of Ernest Thompson Seton*)

We saw the trumpeter swans. We stopped to watch them preen and swim for a while.

Trumpeter Swans

Ernest Seton also used the Charlotte Mason approach of observing a scene from nature, turning away, and narrating what he had seen. He told his boy scouts to look at a scene carefully, close their eyes and recount ten native plants and ten forms of animal life they had observed. This awakened the boys to the rich variety of the wilderness around them.

Other writers, naturalists, and artists take a more refined approach. Edith Holden kept a nature journal which her family treasured for years and has released for publication. Her *Diary of an Edwardian Lady* is a beautiful example of what a nature notebook can be. She concentrates on thoughts about the months and seasons. Her paintings are of a gentler sort than Seton's, depicting mostly birds and leaves. She includes poetry and folk lore.

It is fascinating to study the journals, notebooks, and sketch books of these other travelers. You may experiment with all of their methods. But as you make your own way in the world, your own style and interests will emerge and lead you in your own paths. Follow the paths as your heart leads.

In teaching children the possibilities of discovery journals, it is also helpful to show them examples from this book and those listed in the appendix. It will give them an idea of what has been done before and where they might start. Search the great minds of the past and trace their development in their own words, images, and experiments. Seek out the kindred spirits of our own time and see what you can learn from each other. But most of all, begin your journey with courage. Discover your own path one step at a time, and keep on until the end.

June 28-29th, 1997

We watched a little moth uncurl his proboscis
a sip from deep inside this blossom,
The proboscis was 2 or 3 times the
length of the antena.

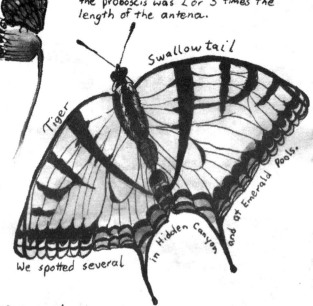

Swallowtail

Tiger

in Hidden Canyon

and at Emerald Pools.

We spotted several

When we came back to Salt Lake I noticed
one right here in Murray Park! Now I know
what it is I will be able to see them again and
again!

This moth was still on the trail. I picked
it up and spread the wings to reveal
the bright underwings. When the
wings are closed blended into the
foliage discreetly.

actual
size

Every child is an artist.
The problem is how to
remain an artist
once he is grown up.

—Pablo Picasso

Chapter 3

JOURNALS FOR EVERYONE

I am excited about journaling because it is something my whole family enjoys together. As soon as the baby can hold a pencil she can begin to explore and record her discoveries with my help. A discovery journal can be kept before the children have acquired the skills of writing necessary for the more traditional journal. It is a good place for children to practice their newly learned skills of drawing, observation, writing and record keeping. Teens can explore their own talents and strengths in the safe place of a journal. They can discover what they want to spend their energies on. As a busy mother I find my journal to be a refuge from my daily cares. It is a place to capture precious moments with my children and the world I love, a way to expand my education and my joy in life's adventure.

My mother and father in their late seventies also enjoy our outings. It renews their spirits if not their bodies. They can reminisce and add their experience to our discoveries. The children love to bring Grandpa a bit of rock, a flower or a berry and hear his stories about the summer when . . . .

Camilla Kimball, a religious women's leader, was once asked why she took up painting when she was in her nineties. She replied that at her age there weren't that many things you could take up and expect to do well, but painting was one of them.

We like to share our journals with other family members. We can learn what captures another's imagination. We find we notice different details. We also go back to them to prove points in family arguments about when the wheat was ripe last year or where the family camped in 1995.

Discovery journals are enjoyable because they engage the senses and the intellect. Everyone is on equal ground when you say "Discover something new today." There is no competition to do better than your brother. There is only a feeling of doing the best you can for today. It is very personal. It is a great way to track your progress in writing, sketching, and personal growth. It is a priceless record of memories that will not be lost or crowded out.

There is very little comparison between children and adults as to quality. Everyone's impressions are equally valid. In practice, it is very rare that anyone chooses to paint the same thing as his brother. And even if they do choose to paint the same flower it will often be from a different perspective or emphasizing different qualities. One time I put a mixed bouquet of flowers in the center of the kitchen table and asked the children to all paint what they saw. Like the blind men and the elephant, everyone saw a different vase of flowers depending on their point of view. We had a wonderful philosophical discussion on how each person sees things a little differently. It was a good lesson for us all.

On another occasion, four of us were so excited to spot a kingfisher at the river that we all tried to paint him. One subject, four painters, four different paintings resulted. There were, of course, comparisons made. We concluded that one boy got the shape just right, another mixed just the right color, another included some habitat, and another included a descriptive paragraph to capture the mood of day. All were informative, expressive and unique. Everyone did excellent work.

I like journaling because it stays put. So much of what I do each day has to be done again the next. The dishes are

complete for only an hour before they must be done again. But when I record something in my journal it stays put. A week or a year later it means more than the day I placed it there. It is one activity that increases in value as time goes by.

Very young children can benefit from the habit of putting their drawings in a notebook rather than on the walls. They also get great enjoyment out of being like their grown-up friends. Young children who have not yet gained the motor skills to write or draw may enjoy keeping a scrapbook of pictures or memorabilia they discover, such as a ticket stub from the zoo with magazine pictures of the animals they like, labeled by Mom. This form of discovery book can be a meaningful activity for little ones. They will spend hours pouring over their pictures and learning to read the words important to them. When your child shows an interest in drawing his own pictures, by all means, encourage him. You can be a great help in writing down his explanation of what he has drawn. You will be glad you took the time later, when you have both forgotten what he was trying to draw.

Charlotte Mason, the British educator, was a great advocate of "nature notebooks" for teacher and students. She suggested that children be encouraged to begin them at about age six. By this age, many children can draw symbolic pictures and are beginning to explore letters and words. Encourage their efforts but do not pressure them. Journals should always be a pleasant experience. They should never be a test or assignment at this age.

Some children feel more comfortable with visual expression while other prefer verbal expression. Let them use the form of communication with which they are most comfortable. Then encourage them to stretch a bit by adding a few words of explanation or a simple sketch to embellish the page. Children who struggle with writing or spelling are often pleased to narrate their thoughts to a parent who can write it neatly on the page for them. This is often a better choice in the formative stages of writing. It removes frustration. It ensures valuable parental involvement. It gives them a chance to express more complex ideas than they might otherwise. Most children have greater speaking vocabularies than writing vocabularies. It gives the parent a chance to discuss the experience with the child and add insight. It gives the children examples of good penmanship to follow. When they are ready to write their own narrations, you will find them doing just that. They will learn to write as naturally as they speak.

On the other hand, I would hesitate to sketch for a child. It is better for them to work through their own artistic stages. They must work through stages of development in art just as they work through the development of large motor skills of creeping, crawling, walking and jumping. It is helpful for the parent to be aware of the major stages in development but not to put any pressure on the child to run before he can crawl. When they are ready for some instruction, they will show signs of frustration or dissatisfaction with their work. Then you will know they are ready for some help. If they are joyful with their work, for heaven's sake, feel the joy.

Children go through recognizable stages in their art. I stress again that these ages may seem typical, but are approximate. It does not matter how long a child explores any one stage. It is merely nice to know they are progressing through them. Each stage has its beauties. Teach them to enjoy the place they are in.

Scribbling is the first stage. The two to four-year- old uses color for pure enjoyment. Their work is not realistic. The results may seem to be disordered and reflect the child 's emotional state. There are no literal

images. They need practice with fine motor skills. This is the time to play with color. Mixing watercolors is a delight.

The *pre-schematic* stage typically ranges from four to seven years. Motor skills are developing. These drawings are beginning to look like something. Symbols begin to evolve for the body, for mother, for the child himself. The objects are not grounded and seem to float in space. Often the same symbol is repeated over and over again. Let them practice their

Self Portrait
Enoch
just turned six

*Pre-schematic stage
ages 4-7*

way through this stage without criticism or censure. Every effort is cause for encouragement and praise.

The *schematic* stage may emerge between seven and nine years of age. Here, the child begins to discover a relationship between color and objects. He will begin to formulate definite concepts of man and his environment. This is a wonderful age

Fallow Deer
Schematic Stage
ages 7-9

to introduce discovery journals. The children are young enough to be receptive and willing to try. Yet, they are not overly concerned about their drawing "looking right." The symbols are still enough, and yet they are beginning to be more sensitive to the color of the sky and the shape of the mountain. At this stage one of my sons painted rainbows repeatedly, always with the colors in their natural order. Another son seemed obsessed with volcanos and lava, enjoying vibrant dramatic colors. My third son began to notice straight lines, curves, and angles, using them to identify animals and landscapes. Don't be surprised if they still resort to scribbles to fill in spaces when tired or frustrated. Some days I get stuck right here when I don't have a clue how to approach a thicket of trees with a pencil.

The next stage is *dawning realism* which may dawn around nine to eleven years of age. The child now wants to draw realistically. She will observe carefully and give more attention to detail. This is a good time to suggest shading figures to help represent shape and texture. She may be receptive to drawing lessons in this stage. You may notice a leap forward in the quality of observation and ability to express shape, volume, and light in their discovery journals. As they discover principles of drawing, they will be pleased with their own improvement.

Dawning realism stage—ages 9-11

Another stage is called *pseudo-naturalistic*. I hesitate to even put an age range on this development. In this stage the artist may experiment with color. He may use it to express emotion or mood or to express a sense of distance. While it may not be as "realistic" as the previous stage, it is the beginning of artistic interpretation and exploration. Let them explore their possibilities freely. A little color theory would be appropriate in this stage.

Pseudo-naturalistic stage (abstract)

The last stage is aptly called the *crisis of adolescence.* I am sure you can guess what happens here. The child's visual perception develops. Their artwork becomes more introspective and personal. Issues of privacy, independence, adequacy, and autonomy will be evident in your child's art as well as their writing, speaking, thinking, and behavior. Be prepared to

Crisis of adolescence stage

guide them through this trying time. It may be helpful to show them their old journals and explain their progress. Explain they are still learning and will continue to learn throughout their life. Explain that excellence is a journey and not a destination. As Michelangelo said, "I am still learning."

Warning: Many a teenage journal has ended up in the trash because they have become embarrassed by their weaknesses. When my daughter turned twelve something came over her all of a sudden. She didn't want to be a child anymore or be known for her childish things. She took her discovery journal, which was perfectly wonderful for an eleven year old and tore out all the pages that were not up to her new standards. Her book, which covered the last two years of her life, was a fraction of itself. I was heartbroken and I think she will be also in twenty years. This is not unusual behavior for a teen. I remember my sister coming home from college on Christmas break her freshman year. She went through all her photos and school annuals, cutting out her picture because she didn't want to look like that any more. So, be forewarned that this crisis may come. Teach your children to enjoy the journey, to be patient with their development, and to recognize change. And, keep their old journals on a high shelf until they marry. Their new spouse will thank you for them.

Many adults have had the experience of becoming blocked somewhere along this journey. In my experience, the biggest road block to artistic expression comes from FEAR. Whenever the child realizes the difference between what she meant to draw and what she did draw and feels a sense of failure because of it, that is where her artistic development stops. For many of us it occurs during the stage of "dawning realism," when we want our drawings to be realistic. The myriad insecurities of pre-adolescence also contribute to FEAR OF FAILURE. It becomes too risky to face failure, so many quit trying. If you quit, there will be no evidence to convict you. Drawing lessons of some sort at this time can give us the tools and techniques to move beyond fear to confidence and a willingness to keep trying. As adults we may need to begin again at the same stage we left off at age ten or eleven and practice our way through these developmental stages. Several adult artists I have known believe that having mastered these stages of development it is also possible to move backward through these same stages as a mature artist to discover one's own best self.

Here are a few books I recommend that discuss artistic development:
> *Drawing on the Right Side of the Brain*
> by Betty Edwards
> *Drawing with Children*
> by Mona Brooks
> *Drawing with Children and Teens*
> by Mona Brooks

Do not think that you need to take classes or training of some sort before you begin. I never was able to fit art classes into my schedule in high school, college, or as a busy mom. I learned to draw by drawing. Much the way I learned to read by reading and learned to cook by cooking. I still have a lot to learn and I do hope that someday I will be able to fit in a class, but in the meantime I will go on practicing. I have also learned many things through books from the library. I suggest that you go through the watercolor and drawing books at your library and check out the ones that appeal to you. Study them as time permits.

Discovery journals are not just about art. They are about writing, too. More people feel comfortable with writing than drawing. There is more concentration in our society on written expression and it is taught more consistently through the school years. Still, many would like to write more than they do. It takes much the same discipline to set aside time to write as it does to set aside time to draw. Our lives are oh, so busy. It takes a little more stretching at the end of a day to write in a journal than to watch the late show. Still, I think the desire is there for many, it just doesn't happen, like so many good things we would like to be doing.

It is helpful to set a goal of writing regularly. Chose a realistic time and place. Write down your goal and post it where you will see it often. Plan for any new habit to take at least six weeks to become established. Tell a loved one of your goal and ask for support. Give yourself a little reward for good behavior. In college I used to write in my journal after a jog and a shower. Now I write during nap time or while the children play. Sometimes the dishes have to wait a bit, but they never disappear. My memories will, if I let them sit too long.

It's nice to have a catch up day every so often. I sometimes take a day to list all the things we've been doing that I haven't had time to write about. Later, if I have the time and inclination I can give more detail. I like to take my journal to doctors' offices because the time passes so quickly while I'm writing. There is no need to feel bored if you have a journal and a pencil.

Older people have a great advantage in journaling. They have traveled farther, seen more, learned more, remember more. They can see connections and patterns that a younger person cannot know. When they draw a robin, they have a whole lifetime of experiences with robins to draw from and write about, remember and cherish. Moreover, the world is so full of wonderful things. It would take many lifetimes to discover them all. My great-grandfather was a devoted journal writer. I love to read his first hand accounts of crossing the plains in a wagon train, riding with the pony express, and what he ate for Sunday dinner. Though I never met him, I feel I know him. I feel connected to my ancestors that left accounts of their doings, where the others are only names and dates.

There is great power in combining a written journal with sketching and painting. For one thing it is more enjoyable to peruse later. Written journals have a tendency to become dull and repetitive, just as our lives sometime become. Pictures, on the other hand, will not be repeated exactly the same. Also, as the saying goes, pictures can be worth a thousand words in describing detailed observations, while words may be more expressive of moods or insights. They are both excellent ways of communicating experience, something we humans often feel a need to do. Painting must be a different kind of thought process, however. It slows me down so I can relax and savor details that I would pass by otherwise. It is a different kind of contemplation.

Perhaps your pictures are awkward or your writing stiff. It doesn't matter. They will both improve with practice. Meanwhile, they can support one another. Together, they will more clearly represent your thoughts, concerns, experiences and discoveries than either one could alone.

In addition, visual expression has a way of helping the words to come more freely. The freedom of sketching some-how loosens the words and helps refine your thoughts so that you can get them on the page. This is a good technique to use with children who have trouble thinking of what to write about. If they can draw a picture, they can write about the pic-ture and tell why it is important to them. If your strengths lean toward words, the sketches can embellish the page with beauty or humor.

Doing journals on wild days has freed my family and I from other inhibiting and stressful attitudes. We don't try to do them every day. That is too hard in our busy lives. It guarantees failure and guilt. Instead, we use them spontaneously on a regular basis. About once every two weeks we are ready for a wild day, a break out from normal routine. Ironically, these are the days we feel are worth remembering and we make the time to record them. I have found great joy in doing this. I know it has built good memories for my children. We enjoy being together. We enjoy the earth with her intricate web of life. We love the Creator of us all.

I asked my family about these experiences. This is how they responded.

Enoch (six years)— *I feel happy when we go on field trips like camp-outs and stuff like that. And when we go to the zoo. I like going down to the river. I like to look for animals like deer. I like to look for wildflowers. I like to come home afterward and paint pictures of what we saw. I like to do it about every two weeks. It's just fun. We get to find out other stuff we didn't know about like finding new trails and exploring places.*

Riley (nine years)— *When we have wild days we usually go places to look at things. We've studied ponds, different birds, animals, butterflies and sometimes we just go to see what we can discover. I like to go to the zoo to see what's going on there. I would like to go to the zoo every other day*

if I could. When you go a lot you learn more about the zoo. You can know where all the animals are. Every single time I've gone, the animals have been doing something different. You can learn more about them and how they behave. I like going up the canyon. The animals in the canyon will be doing more wild things than the ones in the zoo. It's more important to see how they behave in the wild. In the zoo they are more used to people and more tame. They don't have to worry about hunting for their own food. Usually I like to do my journal at home because when I am on field trips I'm involved in other things like going on hikes and exploring the woods and looking at animals. Reading about animals, you don't know if it's true for sure. Different books say different things sometimes. By watching animals you know that whatever they do, their entire species does and they will probably do it more than once.

When we see an animal out in the wild and we don't know what it is, we go home and look it up and do a page in our journal about it. We do that so we can remember it, so we can learn to draw it, and so we will know what it is when we are older. I like to draw pictures in my journal. I like to paint them, color them with crayons and markers. I like to narrate to my mom and have her write down the name of the animal, the measurement, what they were doing, We write down the date, things about the animals like where they live what they eat. When I grow up I would like to be a forest ranger or a zoo keeper and study animals.

Isaac (eleven years)— *I feel like wild days are good because they give us a break from other stuff. We go places that we might not otherwise. It's good to have a wild day about every two weeks. I like that we do our nature notebooks on these wild days. I like having time to look around and decide what to put in my nature notebook. The thing I like the most about nature notebooks is being able to look back at the*

first thing I did and seeing that I have improved in my art work. I like to draw while we are out and then fill in the colors when we come home. I think writing in it is good. You should put the date and label what you saw and tell something you know about it. It helps you to remember the day. I'm not as shy as Riley, and I like to meet people and make friends when we go on outings. I like to get together with them later after I'm done with school. I don't like it when Mom forces us to do our journals. I like to go places with our nature notebooks. Then we can do a page if we feel like it, but we don't have to. I think that people should give their kids freedom to do what they want, but at the same time you should give them suggestions.

Anita (fourteen years)— *I would recommend wild days and nature journals to everyone. Although I don't enjoy doing the journals very much, I still do it because it is good for me.*

My favorite place to go for a wild day is up the canyon. I like it because there is always a new path I haven't explored yet. Once I climbed up a waterfall. I kept hiking for one or two hours. I got to the top of the mountain right about sunset. It was a breathtaking sight.

Nature is the breath of life. It has a strong sense of peace and joy. It is a place where you can think, a place to unload your troubles. A place that is close to God. A place that is necessary for everyone's mental, spiritual, and emotional health.

Mom— *Working with many children at the same time can be challenging. I usually do not try to work in my own journal while I am helping all the children. After an outing, and usually after some food and re-grouping, I will wipe off the kitchen table and bring out the journals. For a few minutes I act as the facilitator, fetching paints, water, or pencils. I will help them identify plants or animals in a field guide or check other reference material. Attention spans vary with the age and mood of the child so we try to use that to our advantage. If we all start together, the six-year-old is usually done first and runs off to play. Perhaps the eleven-year-old is done next. He is quick and to the point, needing little help from me. As they finish their entries I set their books on the kitchen counter to dry and generally try to keep the working space clean. I change paint water for the younger ones, answer the phone or door, answer questions. The nine-year-old may need help with his writing and need some one-on-one time. The thirteen-year-old may read a bit in a reference book while the little ones are splashing paint. About the time the two-year-old is done, the thirteen-year-old will be ready to start. Then she can have the table to herself and do a better job. I may wait till the next day and snatch a few minutes before they all*

get up or a little time after lunch to catch up on my own thoughts.

When we decide to paint in the field, I let the children play first to run off energy. We may hike for a while until something catches our interest or creates a mood. After a time, I will find a bench, a rock, or a shady spot of grass to rest on. While they play and explore, I will sketch, and if time permits, paint. They will bring me their finds, or stories of them. About a half an hour before it is time to go, I warn them that it is nearly time to return home and if they haven't had a chance to paint, they should do so. Sometimes they sketch quickly, promising to finish at home. Other times they will finish their painting and writing right then.

Grandma (seventy-eight years)— *I have a basic need for beauty in my life. I always have. It fills a hole in my life. When I have the chance to see beautiful things and paint I get so excited. I feel like I'm floating on air! I like quiet when I work. I like to be alone to concentrate. I need about a three-hour block of time to get my thoughts down on paper. I have so much to learn.*

Give it a try. If you already keep a journal, try adding some sketches for spice. If you like to draw, get a little note-book where you can keep your sketches together and write about your pictures. If you want to slow down the hectic pace of vacations, take an hour to paint. If your students need some excitement, if your children are bored, if you are wondering what to do with your girl scout troop, take a Wild Day. If you are looking for something positive to lure your children away from electronic screens, take them on an adventure. If you are wild with responsibilities, give yourself a break. Have a Wild Day!

Chapter 4

STARTING YOUR JOURNAL

WHAT MATERIALS DO I NEED?
- — a pencil
- — a spiral-bound journal with heavy weight paper
- — a small watercolor set
- — a black waterproof pen

OPTIONAL SUPPLIES
- — a hand held magnifying glass
- — a small ruler
- — butterfly net
- — water
- — snacks

— field guide books
— binoculars
— a camera
— a knapsack

A knapsack is nice to keep these things together and your hands free while you walk. It is also nice to use a knapsack if the whole family is bringing their supplies.

Start with a regular pencil and a spiral-bound journal with unlined pages. The bound journal helps to keep your papers together safely. It will also give you a record of your progress and some continuity to your discoveries. The spiral binding enables you to lay the journal flat for drawing comfort and to leave it flat while the watercolors dry. I have found the 9" by 6" size good for traveling. It is less intimidating. I can slip it into the large pocket of my winter coat with a pencil and not have to carry a knapsack. (A fishing vest with all of its pockets might be fun in the summer.) Younger children may prefer the larger 8 1/2" by 11" size. It gives more freedom of expression for young ones not ready for detailed work. My mother (seventy-eight years) enjoys working on large pages. The only drawback of the larger size is the weight of the pack if you have several children. I let my children choose whatever they want. Most have opted for the smaller size after trying both. However, one child insists that bigger is better.

You will want to buy a book that has good quality paper suitable for watercolor. I like a heavy weight, durable 80# paper that is suitable for pens, pencils, and watercolor. Sometimes you will want to use a lot of water in your pictures. This can cause thinner paper to buckle or even dissolve. Sometimes you may be caught in the rain. Invariably a cup of paint water will spill at sometime. So it is best to buy a sturdy book.

Next, invest in good quality watercolors. There is a world of difference between cheap paints and established name brand varieties. I like the small Winsor & Newton™ sets that come in a case with a brush or two. Buy a set large enough to include black. Tube paints will last and last if used with care. But pan paints are also good. They may be easier for children or elderly to use since they have no caps to get stuck. It is easy for little fingers to squeeze out more than they need from a tube!

Ask for help at your art supply or craft store. They will probably have many sizes from which to choose. These traveling sets make great Christmas or birthday gifts for older children. (Judge how old they must be when you see the prices!) Crayola™ pan paints are the best I have found for children under eight. They are relatively inexpensive, washable, with clear colors. The sets of eight colors are the best. If you get the larger set, the child will be less apt to experiment with mixing colors. They will learn more from mixing than they will from using the paint straight from the pans. This is the time to teach them how to keep their paints clean and how to mix colors from the three primary colors. Teach them proper brush care. When they have learned how to use their Crayolas™ well, then they will be ready for a more expensive set.

You will need two or three good sable or ox-hair brushes: a small fine point, a medium point, and a medium-sized flat. That should be enough for work on small sketch books. If you have any brushes with plastic bristles, throw them away or use them only for glueing projects. They will only cause frustration. If your good brushes are too long for your paint box, just cut the handle shorter. A sharp point on the end (made with a pencil sharpener) can be handy for rendering quick grasses and tree limbs.

If you take good care of the brushes, they will last for years. Always keep the brushes clean. Don't let paint dry inside the metal casing where the bristles are rooted or your brush will become stiff. And don't let the brushes sit bristle down in the paint water. They will lose their points. Gently reshape the points before they dry with your fingers. The bristles retain the shape they dry in, even after they are placed in water again. If children have their own personal brushes, they will take better care of them.

A black, waterproof, fine tip, permanent pen is great for details and definition. Pick something with which you can build a relationship. My art major roommate in college thought her blue Bic fine point sacred. Technical pens are fun to use and you can pick a size that suits your handwriting and style. I like the .03 size. It is very fine, but not so tiny that the tip will break with heavy use.

That's all you need— paper, a pencil, watercolors, and a black pen!

Just a note about quality. Good materials are expensive but they work so much better and they last a lot longer. You wouldn't buy a toy mixer for your kitchen or a toy saw to build a fence. Don't waste your money or time on inferior tools. (Well, maybe a few cheap sets for the preschoolers to keep them out of the good stuff.)

There are frequent sales on art supplies. Many craft stores run coupons in the newspaper. Some competitor stores will take other store's coupons. Shop around for the notebooks. Some of the superstores carry them for less than art supply stores. Sometimes they include them in their 25%-off-all-stationary sales. It's O.K. to collect supplies slowly. Explore the possibilities of the watercolors first, then add the technical pen. Every so often a new pen or pencil will give your art a boost as you explore its possibilities. Have fun with each new purchase while you wait for the next great deal.

For those of a scientific bent, tuck a magnifying glass and ruler in your backpack. It is useful later to know exactly the dimensions of a blossom or insect. Butterfly nets make insect study easier. Besides, running around with a butterfly net strips away inhibitions!

Drinking water is important on any hike and can also serve as paint water or cleansing water for scrapes or cuts. However, my children don't like to use tap water for their paintings. "Tap water, Mom? Get real! You can't use tap water to paint a river! You have to use river water!" My daughter is quite a romantic. She prefers to use pond water for ponds, rainwater for rain, and melted ice or snow to paint the frozen marsh in January.

1/9/97 Today we went to the park. It was very cold. We played on the equipment for a while, then we played catch.

The park we went to had a maze of small ponds that had up to three inches of ice over only half an inch of water. We walked on the top of the ice, cracking it up a lot. Everybody got very muddy. I painted this picture in gloves, using a piece of ice for water.

—Anita, 13 years.

If bad weather dampens your enthusiasm for nature study, keep in mind a few alternatives. Museums are a good choice. Nature videos might be a back-up plan. Nature crafts are also enjoyable on dreary days. We keep a treasure box full of things the children have brought home from outings. On rainy days we can go to the treasure box and pull out a stone, a snake skin, or a few pine cones to paint in our journals. On rainy days we seem to have more time for research and careful drawings.

2 May 1997,

Don't rule out public places altogether. When the weather is threatening the crowds thin out. Our zoo has many of its animals housed in buildings. The reptiles, the butterflies, the hippos, the big cats, even the elephants have enclosures to protect them from inclement weather. The children love to run from building to building in the rain. On one outing it began to snow. The zoo quickly became deserted. It was so quiet, so peaceful. We watched the polar bear romp and swim in the swirling flakes with her cubs. That was a day to remember.

Snacks make the journey more enjoyable. They are good rewards for encouraging young ones to write or paint. They can give everyone a boost when the trail back seems a lot longer than the trail out. Be careful not to leave any litter. I often leave the snacks in the car so I don't have to carry them. The litter is then more controllable. They also give me a reward to lure the children back. Some of my children would adventure on into the night if their stomachs did not call them home.

One year we tired of buying expensive little building sets for our boy's birthday. Knowing he loved exploration and nature, my husband decided to get him binoculars instead. I wasn't sure an eight-year-old would appreciate the gift, much less care for it properly, but I was wrong. This shy boy is always the most popular one on our family hikes because we are all trying to get a peek from his field glasses when we spot wildlife. He is careful with them and values them highly. We use them frequently in the home also. There is a wide variety in price and quality of field glasses. Find a helpful clerk and explain what your requirements are. We explained to our clerk that it was for a child and needed to be easy to focus. The pair we bought for Riley have been wonderful and cost about twenty-five dollars.

Our bird feeders are only ten feet from the kitchen table through a large window. With the binoculars we can sit at the kitchen table and see incredible detail on the finches and hummingbirds that come to feed. We can watch the robins play in the cherry trees from the bedrooms unnoticed. Our neighbor has a large yard which he keeps partially *el naturale,* i.e. in weeds. In the winter and early spring, flocks of starlings and cowbirds, come to feed on the weed seeds. One day we saw movement out in the grasses but were not sure what it was. The field glasses revealed tiny baby finches feasting on the white dandelions. The birds were just the same size as three balls of fluff.

Many people have asked me why we don't just take pictures. Cameras record your experiences instantly with less fuss. I do take a camera on some outings but the benefits of photography are so completely different from nature sketching that they really are apples and oranges to one another. In photography you are concentrating on composition, framing, focus, light and distance. You snap the shot and move on. Sketching takes more time. You study your subject in more detail. Why is it that color? What makes it unique? You philosophize about its nature. You notice details, sounds, smells, shapes, weather conditions, spirit.

> As Georgia O'Keefe explains,
> *Nobody sees a flower—*
> *Really it is so small it takes time—*
> *We haven't time-*
> *And to see takes time,*
> *Like to have a friend takes time.*

The colors are really much different in person than they are in a photograph. The feeling is different. By the time I get

Moriah—3 years

the picture back from the developer, I have forgotten why I took it. The photos may capture a certain beauty and feeling, but it will be a different beauty and feeling than a sketch or painting. I like both, but I learn more from painting.

A photo will record a certain surface reality, the truth for an instant. But a drawing can capture a broader truth just because it takes longer and more contemplation is involved. When our youngest child was born we took lots of pictures of her. But the most expressive portrait we have of her first few months is this drawing by her seven-year old brother. Her true nature shines through.

A tote bag or knapsack is handy for keeping your supplies together. We keep ours by the kitchen table. Then it's all ready to go anytime the need arises for a Wild Day. When we come home, it goes back by the kitchen table because often that night or the next day we will want to put finishing touches on a picture or add some comment about the outing. It's easy to grab a field guide or reference book once we are home to see if we can identify the mushroom or insect we saw along the way.

There are so many field guides available that I find it hard to choose. Certainly it is good to have one for your immediate locale. Some are made from photographs while others use drawings and paintings. Both have their advantages. Photographs can look exactly like the wildflower. But field guide paintings emphasize the distinguishing features. This can be useful in identifying birds. Small guides are good for packing with you. I leave my larger comprehensive guides in the car or on the shelf at home to refer to later. One of my goals is to have my drawing or description clear enough that I will be able to identify the subject later from a field guide.

I also enjoy researching a little folk lore and usage. One day we all painted a mushroom that popped up in the lawn. That night we identified it as an Inky Black mushroom and read that it was sometimes used for ink. We couldn't wait to try it out the next day. By the next morning the mushroom was in its black drippy stage. My daughter carefully collected the drips and made another painting. The painting was wonderfully expressive but unfortunately we could not keep it. It smelled just like rotting fungus!

Of course, there are many other art supplies that may work well for you. Natural products expand the imagination. Berry juice is fun to try. A blackened stick from a campfire may help you get in touch with your primitive self. Some folks like colored pencils or drawing pencils. If they work for you, use them! I save my nice Prismacolor™ and watercolor pencils for home use. If I take them outside I invariably lose the color most needed in the long grass aside the trail. I choose watercolor and ink because it is the quickest way to capture a fleeting image with permanence.

Pencils, crayons, or pastels will smear. You can prevent this by spraying your drawing with a fixative. It comes in a can like spray paint and has similar warnings of health hazards. But it does allow you to preserve your drawing without smudging. You can even rework it or add to it after spraying. But, I don't like packing the can around. I try to keep my backpack as light as possible. I don't want to carry around a whole studio. A #2 pencil and a notebook slipped in a pocket is all I can handle some days! I want freedom!

RECORDING THE EXPERIENCE

Now you have the supplies of your choosing tucked in a pocket or knapsack. It's time for the experience. Many journal writing programs used in schools and homes fail for the simple reason that "There is nothing to write about." So, go out and do something! Go to the zoo, walk around the block, run in the park, drive to the canyon or beach, discover a wild place. Play. Charlotte Mason advised her students to spend large amounts of time in the wild, summer and winter. After a few hours of play, exploration, and adventure you will surely have something to remember. Don't try to document everything. Just jot down the date, the weather, the time of day, and one thing you noticed, a pine cone, a bird, your shifting moods. Add a sketch. Do it again the next week, and the week after that.

Remember, whatever you choose to do with your journal is fine. Lab notes, a personal geography, a field guide to your home on Willow Street, a sketch book or volumes of jam writing, it's all O.K. You will learn from them all. You are in charge. You decide what you want. It is the doing that is important, not the final form.

John Muir, the founder of the Sierra Club, wisely wrote, "When we try to pick out anything by itself, we find it hitched to everything else in the Universe." (*My First Summer in the Sierra, 1911*) This is very true of discovery journals. The art is hitched to the science, which is hitched to our hearts through personal thoughts woven together by writing.

A journal is not a finished piece of art. It is not a polished literary form. It is a tool for learning, a springboard to other things. A journal can be anything from a confessional to a grocery list. Journals can hold scientific analysis and the poems of a lovesick school girl. Columbus kept both a ship's log and a personal journal. Taken together they explain more about the man and his adventure than either one could alone. Do not try to please an authority or fit into a mold. This is your tool for learning. You may use it as you see fit.

THE BLANK PAGE

Sometimes when you face the BLANK PAGE your mind goes blank as well. We are all intimidated from time to time with the clean untouchable purity of the BLANK PAGE. The first mark I make is a commitment— a visible extension of who I am. And who am I, today?

Once I filled a whole journal with nature notes. It was a record of two years of outings, expressions, discoveries, and joy. I happily made an index on the last pages and bought a new Blank book. I was so excited to make a beautiful creation that the book sat on my shelf for two months! Why? The BLANK PAGE overcame me! So I sat myself down one day and told the BLANK PAGE it was only paper. If I wanted to, I could tear it up. I could throw it in the trash. I could burn it if necessary. It was, after all, only paper. That day I took back my power to act and wrote a date at the top of the page. "May 3, 1997." It was a good start.

Fear has a way of smothering sparks of inspiration. It can paralyze noble action. It can flatten the peaks of our soul. I have heard so many people say,

"But, I've never drawn anything before."

Well, now is a good time to start.

"But, it won't be any good."

Maybe, but then again it might. And we know the Blank Page is no good.

"My sister/mother/uncle is the artist in the family."

Well, maybe there are two of you.

"I have no talent."

Talent is just another word for work.

"People will laugh."

The world needs more laughter.

"I like to draw and/or write, but I could never show my work to anyone."

That's O.K. This is for you. It is personal. It is unique. Only you can decide when it is right to share your heart with another.

You have probably figured out that this section is for adults only. Children do not have a problem with "The Blank Page." They know they are in charge. They have only themselves to please. They know it will be fun. Every new adventure is fun. They know the page has no value unless it holds their creation. The product is not important, only the experience. Let me say that again. THE PRODUCT IS NOT IMPORTANT, ONLY THE EXPERIENCE.

Open yourself up to the adventure of discovery. Let your children, your grandchildren, your tiny neighbor friends teach you how to create for the joy of it. (And they will think your efforts are wonderful. Just as you think theirs are.)

Start with the date at the top of the page. It transforms your drawing or painting, description or poem into a finite expression of the day. You are not recording the universe as you know it. You are merely trying to capture one small nugget of a golden day, a memento that you can take out to examine later on a day that may not be as bright. You will be glad you did.

7 July 1997
1:30 p.m. hot

Rattlesnake on the Path in
the Fairywood
at Red Butte

Dragonfly
at Red Butte

Damselfly

37

One learns by doing a thing;
for though you think
you know it,
you have no certainty
until you try.

—Sophocles

Chapter 5

TEACHING ART THROUGH DISCOVERY JOURNALS

Art is perhaps the easiest academic application of discovery journals. Call it an artist's sketch book. One wet day we went to a natural history museum to look at the specimens and sketch. What did we find? A college art class sprawled on the floor of the museum sketching. My children commented, "Hey Mom, I guess we're doing college work now." And so they were. If you feel unsure of where to begin, begin simply. You don't need a masterpiece the first day. You don't need to record everything you see. Just start.

I like to begin my journal workshops with painting a leaf. Any leaf. You choose. Leaves have simple symmetrical shapes. John Ruskin said "If you can paint a leaf you can paint the whole world." It is a place to start. Sketch the shape first with a pencil. If even this seems intimidating, you can trace it or, if the sun is bright, shadow trace. Hold the leaf a bit above the paper and trace it's shadow as it falls on the page. Children love this. Next, play with your paints until you capture the very color of that individual leaf. Fill in your outline. If the color seems to fade or change as it drys, add another glaze of color over the dry paint. Or, wet the shape with green paint and add a drop or two of yellow color. Let the paint do the work while you get familiar with its temperament. While the paint is wet, add vein lines with a fingernail or the pointed end of your brush. The pigment will settle in the etched line a bit darker than the rest of the leaf. Add any distinctive feature that makes your leaf unique— a curling stem, some insect damage. Now you have captured this leaf. It is yours forever. It gives you a standard by which to compare all leaves. You have finished your first lesson in live nature painting, drawing, color mixing, glazing, wet-on-wet technique, etching, and observation. All in five minutes! Do you like your leaf? Do you want to try another?

People often ask me how I learned to paint with watercolors. I have to choke back an incredulous laugh when I realize they are asking a sincere question. I want to laugh because I know better than anyone that I don't "know how" to paint. I just keep trying new things. Sometimes they work and sometimes they don't.

Every artist is self-taught. I learn how to paint by painting. And I will never be done learning. Remember even Michelangelo said that he was not done learning. I value my mistakes as well as the happy accidents that watercolorists court. I like to look back over my journals and see my development. The first time I painted a rose, well, it sort of looked like a rose, but I labeled it just to be sure I would remember. A year later I tried again. It was better. I figure that if I paint a rose every June for the next twenty years I'll be able to paint a pretty good rose someday. In my living room hangs a watercolor rose that a friend painted. I look at that rose and say to myself, "Someday I'll be able to paint a rose like that." Then I have to remember that she gave me this rose only because she felt she had painted a better one.

On the road to excellence, some are further along than others. Some run by me while I poke along. It seems I have always had a two-year-old in tow. We have to stop and look at every bug and dandelion along the way. As long as I'm headed in the right direction, always observing, always trying to do better, I will improve, albeit slowly. When I get to the end of the road I hope to have my children with me even though we won't be the first to finish. Don't worry about where you are on the road. Just start where you are and move along.

Learning to draw and paint in your journal is a natural process. There are so many things in nature that are difficult to describe in words— the color of a robin's egg or the pattern of a lizard. Drawing the shape of a bird's beak helps to identify it later in a field guide. Pictures are worth a thousand words in identifying unfamiliar plants or the color of the sun on an Irish setter's fur. You will naturally want to learn how to record your observations more exactly. That desire alone will help your art progress over time. Beatrix Potter wrote, "I don't want lessons, I want practice." It is often better to discover your own style slowly by what pleases the spirit within you than to try to please a "teacher". The creative spirit within you will be your best teacher. Beatrix Potter explained, "Thank goodness my education was neglected and the originality was not rubbed off." Be as patient with yourself as you are with your children. Their every effort is a delight. And your efforts can be also.

The process of drawing and painting refine your sense of sight. The more you sketch the more you see. One day at the zoo I realized I was looking at the peacock with new eyes. Hundreds of times I have marveled at the peacock's showy tail-feathers. Nevertheless, after painting birds in my journal, I found myself looking at the incredible texture of his feet, wondering how I could capture that on paper. My children are much more observant of texture and color and shape than they used to be. The artist's eye improves with practice. Artists see things the rest of the world passes by.

I should note that I love to read books about drawing and painting. I love to study the paintings of the masters. When my children were small, we often looked at art books for bedtime instead of the typical children's fare. Of course, the art in children's books has become exquisite now. Go to the art shelves in the library. Check out books with appealing style. Have fun with this visual exploration. Take a class or

July 15ᵗʰ 1998
Yellowstone
Flowers

talk to artists in the park. Remember that you don't need to know much to start, you just need to start. Remember that all you know will not make a difference unless you begin to practice.

There is no need to follow a sequence in learning to draw or paint. Go where your heart takes you. I like wild flowers, trees, and leaves because they don't run 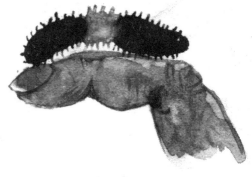 away, the colors are beautiful, and it helps me to learn their names if I paint and label them. However, my husband observed in looking over my notebook that it became more interesting to him when I started painting higher on the food chain: caterpillars, birds, chipmunks.

An advocate of Charlotte Mason's educational philosophies despaired that her children did not want to do nature notebooks. This mom had explained the concepts of drawing and writing about field adventures and started her own book of mostly wild flowers. Her three boys shrugged their shoulders and ran off to play in the undeveloped area behind their house. One day her son reported seeing a quail there. She gently suggested he record his finding in his nature notebook. He liked the idea and drew a beautiful bird. Then he went on to draw beetles and bugs, things that interested him. A ten-year-old boy may struggle to muster much enthusiasm over wild flowers. Still, should he discover a lizard or praying mantis, now then, that may be worth a work of art!

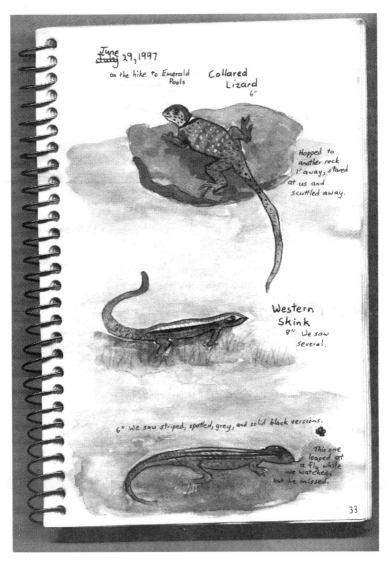

June 29, 1997
on the hike to Emerald Pools

Collared Lizard
6"

Hopped to another rock 1' away, stared at us and scuttled away.

Western Skink
8" We saw several.

6" We saw striped, spotted, grey, and solid black versions.

This one leaped at a fly while we watched, but he missed.

33

Naturalists have often expanded their studies to include dead animals as well. The bird the cat brings home and lays on your step, the deer brought down during the annual fall hunt, even trophy pieces offer an opportunity to study an animal in close detail. I have heard it argued that drawing such a figure can extend the life of the creature through art. Intellectually that may be true. And I suppose death can help to define life. Nevertheless, I have never steeled myself to draw a dead thing. I love life, especially life in the natural world as God designed it. That is what I prefer to study. If my subject runs away before I am through, I can always consult books and photographs.

Our pet hamster died not long ago. I had not made the time to paint him in life, and considered drawing him before the backyard funeral. But it was just too sad. His little body did not look the same in death, the lungs collapsed, the eyes dull. I did not want to remember him that way. No, I would rather do a memory drawing of his cheeks stuffed with baby carrots. One day we all sat around the kitchen table feeding him bits of broccoli. He quickly grabbed every bit of broccoli offered and stuffed it in his cheeks. We laughed and laughed as his face grew rounder and the skin stretched tight. He saved far more in his cheeks than he could eat. When we put him back in his cage, he hid most of it in a corner of shavings for future snacks. I want to remember him that way.

When studying a particular artist, we like to do a picture for our journal in his or her style. Sometimes we copy one of their works that we have been studying. Copying Van Gogh's sunflowers in thick globby paint or creating a Picasso portrait makes those artistic styles stick. They anchor the artist in our memories. Artistically

it is a good way to understand technique and stretch your skills too.

If you are having trouble deciding what to draw because there is too much visual information, try making a rectangle with your hands to frame your picture. This is also a good way to decide on a focal point or to balance your picture. Children enjoy using an empty slide mount as a view finder. Try taking a walk with an empty slide mount in your hand. See how many great compositions you can find.

Try making a thumbnail sketch. This is a sketch the size of your father's thumbnail. It is just big enough to plan out your picture on the page and define values in preparation for a more careful study. Or, you can use a little detailed sketch in the corner of your picture to add information — like a close up of a seed pod when your picture is of the whole plant, or a sketch of the whole meadow where the flower is growing. These insert sketches add a lot of interest and information about your subject.

If you are drawing a close-up of a flower, bird, leaf, or animal it is a good idea to include a habitat sketch with the drawing. Even if the sketch is thumbnail size, it will help you remember where you spotted that bird or how big the tree was where you found the leaf.

Drawings look more realistic if you have a definite light source. Decide which face of your object is in direct light and which is in shade. Add a shadow at the base of the object as indicated by the direction of light. My daughter's pictures took a leap forward when I explained this technique to her of adding shadows.

Foregrounds are usually darker in value than backgrounds. Try making your horizon pastel and the closer flowers or animals in dark, rich colors.

Have you ever wondered why the cartoon artist holds his thumb up beside his picture and squints? There is a reason. You can use your thumb or pencil to help you in many ways. For example, finding angles between trees, measuring relationships between the height of a tree and a hill, or lining up

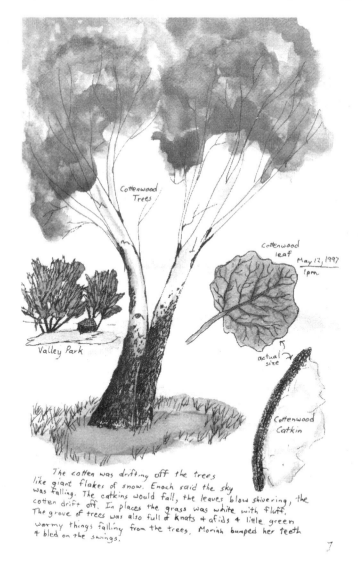

Cottenwood Trees

Cottenwood leaf   May 12, 1997   1pm.

Valley Park

actual size

Cottenwood Catkin

The cotten was drifting off the trees like giant flakes of snow. Enoch said the sky was falling. The catkins would fall, the leaves blow shivering, the cotten drift off. In places the grass was white with fluff. The grove of trees was also full of knots + afids + little green wormy things falling from the trees. Moriah bumped her teeth + bled on the swings.

7

the eyes in a portrait. These tricks are very useful in translating the visual world into the flat plane of the paper. Hold up your thumb at arms length and compare it to the pine tree on the hill. The pine tree may be half a thumb while the hill is two thumbs. When you draw that on your paper you can make the tree exactly one-half thumb and the hill two thumbs.

You can also estimate the height of a tree by measuring its pencil height in proportion to your distance from the tree. In drawing eyes, hold your pencil horizontally across the subject's eyes. If the pencil is not level, the eyes will look odd. For angles, line up the pencil along the straight lines of the object, let's say an old fence post. The angle of the pencil to the ground will be easier to analyze than the angle of the fence post covered in ivy with a squirrel on top.

One more bit of advice for drawing in the field, shade your page with your hat when you are drawing in strong sunlight. The glare from the white page will make it difficult for you to see your subject as you glance back and forth.

Only introduce one of these new ideas to your children at a time. Whether the interval between lessons is two weeks or twenty minutes is irrelevant. They will lose their curiosity and willingness to try if bombarded with more new information than they can try at once. It is better to let them practice their new skills until they are comfortable with them before giving them another concept to think about. Always teach line upon line, precept upon precept. Give yourself this same grace to learn a step at a time. You will improve steadily this way.

You should try out new techniques yourself, before you try to teach them to others. Then you will be able to show them instead of tell them. You may find they don't work and would therefore be frustrating. I sometimes ask my older teens to figure out a technique by experimentation (something like leaf prints that take a little practice) and then teach me and the little ones how to do it. This saves me time and the little ones frustration. It gives the teens much desired respect and autonomy.

Adding new materials to your craft or art supplies can renew lagging interest. Half way through the summer my daughter's interest waned in pressing flowers. A different book from the library awakened her mind to new possibilities. A few days later she left a lovely pressed flower arrangement on my night stand. A week later I brought home a selection of pretty parchment papers from the craft store and was rewarded with an excited squeal.

Teach yourself and your children to observe carefully and describe distinctly. Practice picture painting in your mind. Observe the scene so carefully and with such detail that you can close your eyes and still see the picture. Now you can re-create the scene with your paints from your mind. Developing this capacity to observe, recall information, re-create and describe is a wonderful life skill.

19 May, 1997

We saw a lovely family of Canadian geese at Murray park today. The river was very full from spring run off. It reflected the new green of the cottonwood trees and grass because the sky was white with stratus clouds. The Mama fed with her children on insects in the weeds while

Papa kept a constant lookout, his head always fell and watch. He would let us venture as close as 15 feet, then quietly nudge his family a ways off down the river's edge.

*He must learn to describe
clearly what he has
heard or seen, to transfer
to written language
his sense-impressions
and to express concisely
his own thoughts.*

—*Charlotte Mason*

Chapter 6

LANGUAGE ARTS AND WRITING SKILLS

A s you learn to make your pictures more beautiful, it is natural to want your writing to become more beautiful also. Beautiful handwriting is an art in itself. Experiment with your penmanship and study the work of others. Practice many different styles until your own style emerges in a comfortable beautiful way. Italic printing and hand writing is a good place to start. Both children and adults can learn it easily. It is a simple readable form. It is easy to dress up for formal occasions but casual enough for daily use. Try writing your Latin labels in a different script from your descriptive passages. Put a few frills on your titles. Try writing around, between, or through your pictures for a different effect. Play a lot. Have fun. Make your writing beautiful, personal, unique. Dress up your thoughts.

Gray Jay
or
Camp Robber

L 10"

Perisóreus canadénsis

Writing is much like art in many ways. The world is so large. Where does one start? What do we write about? We must go back to Thoreau and simplify, simplify. That is one strength of the journal. It breaks down our writing into moments that we can manage in a few minutes. We don't need to write about all of life. We can capture our lives, day by day, moment by moment, like the pearls in a necklace.

Sometimes we don't know how things will connect at first. If you feel moved, write it down anyway. The connections will come later, perhaps in a week, perhaps in ten years.

Some people like to keep separate journals for special purposes. A garden journal, a book of quotations, a nature notebook, a spiritual journal, a writer's journal, a record of expenses and expenditures—all are valuable. It makes sense to integrate your journal to include all the aspects of your life, if you are interested in the flow of your life and how experiences enfold. Nevertheless, there are good reasons for compartmentalizing also. My daughter's discovery journal is mostly art renditions of her wild days. She knows I often share her book with others at workshops and parent groups. I always ask her permission. She has always granted it. Her school writing is also open to me for advice and help on occasion. However, she also keeps a totally private journal that I respectfully decline from reading, despite the temptation. Expressive writing, writing that reveals the self, deserves privacy and trust. The pages of a journal can be as revealing as a physician's exam. Likewise, it should be permitted only with permission.

Give yourself a little block of time, five minutes, fifteen. Maybe you will fit it in once a day, once a week, once a month. It doesn't matter. Don't limit yourself with a daily printed diary. You know what I mean, the kind with four lines a day no matter the kind of day and a date printed on the page to accuse you of sloth every time you skip a week. Blank books are better. Date each entry as you make it. Whatever you do write will flow together over time. You will discover themes that may run on for decades or only days. It may seem that such sporadic writing will not maintain continuity. Not so. This is not essay writing with a beginning, middle, and end. This is living writing. A living book. Your book.

A mystery, an adventure, a romance, a quest, a life. Savor it one moment at a time. Be patient while the story unfolds. Chapters will open and close. Perhaps it will have a surprise ending. We can guess, we can plan, we can predict, but we will never know the ending until the last page.

A discovery journal is an excellent way to develop writing skills. Begin by labeling the bird or flower and placing the date on the page. Latin names for plants and animals are interesting. They often lead you to a greater understanding of the object, its distinguishing characteristics, perhaps the history of its discovery, or its folk lore.

Descriptive passages are the next step in expressing your experience on the page. Nothing exists in isolation. The habitat of the animal, a description of its actions, the weather and temperature are all part of a careful description. The colors, the light, your mood may all be part of your experience. Perhaps the moment should be placed in a historical context.

July 3, 1995. We went to Red Butte Gardens. . . . It was beautiful. We saw so many things and hiked so far along the river and up the mountain we didn't have time to paint. We saw a black rabbit, squirrels, ducks, deer tracks, nameless flowers and some that we could name. I was excited to see Sego lilies growing wild on the mountainside. I heard stories of these when I was a child. But I have never seen our state flower in bloom before. In 1910 the school children of Utah voted it the state flower because it kept the pioneers alive in the starving time of 1848. They ate the bulbs.

Also, consider the feeling this descriptive passage captured in my twelve-year-old daughter's journal.

The black sky roars in fury and the helpless ground shudders. The clouds wail and shoot down hot wet darts upon the earth. Pouring down in curtains the raindrops fall, shattering the pavement, whipping the trees and flooding the grass. Children scream and run when the unmerciful lighting flashes. And after a heart splitting crack of thunder, there is a moment of deadly silence.

When writing about an outing or event, include your feelings about what happened. What was your mood? Why? You may think you will never forget, or that the writing implies your feelings, but it is better to record than try to remember. Without emotion your journal will be bland. Let your passions speak out and tell who you are!

Poetry is a natural companion to nature's bounties. So many of our famous poets wrote about the natural world. "Sweet is the lore that Nature brings" —*Wordsworth*. "Morns are meeker than they were" —*Dickenson*. "Nature's first green is gold, her hardest hue to hold" —*Frost*. "One feather is a bird, I claim; one tree, a wood; In her low voice I heard more than a mortal should" —*Roethke*. These poets pepper my journal.

And certainly we should include original poetry too. Paint your pictures with words in a poetic form. The challenge of shaping words into thoughts and literary form is a wonderful intellectual exercise. Flex those brain muscles and write a sonnet when the muses whisper to you.

The Sun—July 1985

In spring the gentle warmth is welcome lace
Lying down on the dark white of winter
With promised flowers of patterned grace.
The rain runs down gentle, the sun splinters,
Those rainbows of life soak down to the
    ground. These seeds

They swell and spring forth with faith and
    thank you's.
Nourished by earth, the browns blossom
    and green.
The living heaven brightens to brilliant
    blues.
Days grow hot and nights are full of star
    song
And crickets fid'ling stories to the moon.
Even star shine seems warm and bright and
    strong
Tomorrow's heat will come so soon so soon
The summer sun will come through lighted
    leaves
The steaming grass, green fire in the melting
    trees.

Many people are afraid to write, afraid of exposure to an unfeeling crowd. Insensitive criticism of expressive writing will seriously inhibit any future writing in children and adults. Criticism has no place in journal writing. If anyone were to share their inner most soul with you the only appropriate response is "Thank you." This is not the place to learn punctuation. It should be a safe place for feelings and ideas, whatever they may be.

You must have experiences you feel strongly about to make the writing worthwhile. Your interest and excitement must come through to the reader. Many daily journals fail to become living books because they are a duty or assignment. I have encouraged all my children to write journals since they were small with varied success. I have learned that it makes an enormous difference when they are given the freedom to write about what is important to them.

For example, on my third son's ninth birthday he left his journal where his seventeen-year-old brother, Nathan, noticed it. The older one exclaimed how interesting it was. He pulled out his own journal which he had kept when he was nine. The difference was pronounced. The older one's entries read "Today we went to the park. It was fun." "Today our friends came over. It was fun." At the same age, Riley's journal reads quite differently.

We were driving through the desert. There were Joshua trees, sagebrush and a hot boiling sun. There were mountains covered with Joshua trees and sagebrush. There was one great big freeway going straight through the middle of the

I would like to go to the desert to camp. I would like to bring a kitchen, so I wouldn't have to hunt.

73

desert. This is a desert tortoise. We also went to the ocean. We saw birds: pelicans, seagulls, cormorants. We saw whales. There were some sea lions. We found some seashells. That was a vacation to California.

These boys have very similar minds and abilities. The difference, I'm sure, was that Nathan's journal was an assigned chore while Riley's journal records his wild days, real life adventures, discoveries and joy. Like the boys in Peter Pan, he recalls his Happy Thoughts and puts them in his journal for safe keeping.

Think of writing as capturing moments of wonder and awe. Record life's little blessings like the color of acorns in the sun or the smell of bread in the oven. These little treasures can put troubles into perspective. They can give us breathing room on a busy day. Record your feelings. Explain why these things are important or significant. If you can write about why you need a "wild day" it may help you sort through those confusing emotions. And be sure to explain what you love to do on your wild days.

Jam writing is another good writing tool for journals. Take a moment and write down everything you are feeling, seeing, sensing, touching, or thinking right now. Where does this lead you? Let the words pour out for at least ten minutes. Where did you travel to? Where did you end up?

Nature has so much to teach us. Look for natural metaphors, symbolic expressions of an inner truth. Write about your natural explorations in the world and in your heart. You will learn more than you think you know. Natural images that capture your imagination may do so for a purpose. Like the Navaho Vison Quest, natural images can teach us beyond our ability to know. Even if you don't understand these images now, they may come to mean more to you in the future. It is your personal symbolic language.

July 2, 1997

Barn
Swallows

6"

Barn swallows are found all over the country. We saw them in Zions, at Red Butte, and again at the old Gardner Mill.

This mother had set her youngster on a post by the Mill pond that was just the same color as his breast.

He hid there quite effectively while she brought him food. He must have been a teenager— not much use, with an enormous appetite. They were nearly the same size. In another week I'm sure she will think he is big enough to fend for himself and work off some of that baby fat.

Chapter 7

SCIENCE AND MATHEMATICS

I was asked to teach a science class one term to a group of reluctant students of mixed ages. The first day I asked them to tell me what they had been doing in their science class. They groaned and obediently pulled out science notebooks full of dull work sheets on plant growth and solar systems. The teacher herself said I would have my work cut out for me to keep the attention of these kids.

First, I told them we would do no more work sheets. They sat up a little straighter in their chairs. I told them that we would do science like real scientists, through our own observations and experiments. They gave each other sideways glances of disbelief. Next, I told them we were going to start right away and they should get their coats. Grins broke out on their faces and they rushed to do my bidding. Armed with a pencil and a piece of paper, the students went out into the school yard with the assignment to find something interesting from nature to study and draw. One half hour later we went back inside and I collected the papers.

The next time we met we went through their pictures and I asked each one to explain their picture and why they had chosen that object to study. Well, they couldn't stop telling me all they knew about dandelions and rain puddles, dinosaurs (one boy was sure he saw one), rain clouds, seagulls, and the cut on John's finger. Then I told them science was over. Groans. "But we never did science!" one little girl complained. I replied that we had spent the last half hour doing science. "But you never taught us anything." "No," I replied. "You were the teachers."

As a group, their interests were varied enough to cover the curriculum. We could study birds for Bobby's week, the moon for Marjorie, and so on as they took turns choosing an interest. I continued to have them first observe, then draw and write about their observations. Later, we hypothesized, tested, observed, then documented our discoveries with pictures and descriptions of what they had learned. Unwittingly, they were creating their own work sheets and textbook. Instead of filling in blank spaces, they were writing the whole text. The spirit of discovery, the habit of observation, and the discipline of recording the facts taught them more than science. Science became more to them than a work sheet you did in school. Many Mondays they greeted me with happy shouts. Waving a drawing in front of me, they yelled, "Teacher, look what I learned this weekend!" Their discovery notebooks became precious indeed.

It may seem that science and math would not find their way into discovery journals. Nevertheless, they do. Scientists call their journals Lab Notes and fill them with formulas and equations that may be indecipherable to the lay person. Still, the habit of recorded experiences or experiments is as valuable to the scientist as the artist or writer. Riley is really not a verbal child. His gifts run more with numbers and logic. His discoveries fascinate me because we think differently.

One day we went to the park in winter and there wasn't much wildlife about. I still encouraged the children to discover one interesting thing. After a while I called the children together to see what they had found. Riley had drawn a pine branch and written in the margin. "This twig has fifty-one needles." I counted the needles on his drawing and the twig and, sure enough, fifty-one were there. We started counting other needle clusters and discovered that they always occurred in odd numbers! How interesting! We wondered why that would be so. I have such respect for his mind and interests. It would never have occurred to me to count the needles on a twig.

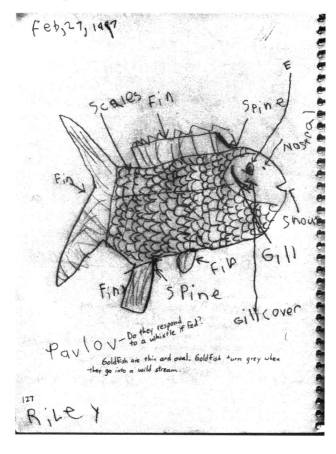

On the other hand, I find myself thinking a lot about color, trying to paint the grays in the heavy snow clouds. Both activities have their value. By letting myself and my children explore our own interests and share with each other how we

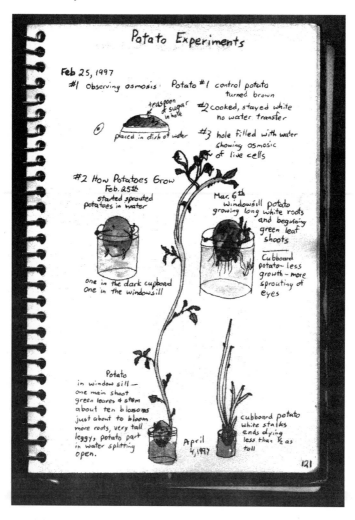

think about the world, we discover more about ourselves and each other. The exercise of sharing our perceptions through words and art is particularly enriching for those not naturally inclined in that direction. Riley's verbal skills have grown tremendously as he tries to translate his impressions into words. We all need to know how to communicate even if it is not our first love.

With my own children we have used our notebooks to chart weather, diagram the parts of a flower, a fish, a bird, and various seed pods. We have used them to measure and record the development of a potato plant. We have written about comets and stars. We have gone to the ocean and listed all the sea creatures we observed. We have recorded the footprints of a hamster, a cat, and a bird. We have studied the phases of the moon and the changes of the seasons. We have looked into a microscope and recorded the image. And we have studied the journals of scientists. Many scientific discoveries were first written down in personal diaries. Leonardo Da Vinci's diaries are a good example. He wrote and sketched about such a diversity of interests that his notes are appealing to many sorts of people.

Several years ago I became interested in recording birds in my journal. I knew the names of a very few birds from my childhood home in San Diego. I wanted to learn the names of birds native to my new home in the Rocky Mountains. Each time my children or I discovered a new bird in our yard or at our favorite parks, I recorded it in my discovery journal. So far I have painted thirty birds! I have enjoyed this so much. They become my friends and I recognize them the next time we meet. My children learn also from my efforts. They love to find a new bird to paint. My six-year-old no longer shouts, "Mommy, a bird!" He squeaks, "Look, Mommy, a starling, a hawk, a chickadee."

Sometimes the artist and the scientist work together to discover new territory. Because I have been interested in painting birds in my journal, I have tried to record all the visitors in my neighborhood. I find I can remember their names and habits better after doing this. Last summer we went on a trip to Zion's National Park in southern Utah. We always enjoy seeing how many new animals and birds we can identify on our trips away from home. On this trip we spotted a beautiful little red bird. We searched our field guide to find its name. We felt it must have been a Summer Tanager but the guide said that its habitat range was further south than we were. There really was no other bird that fit its description. When we went to the Nature Center at the park I asked a ranger if she knew of Tanagers in that area. She was excited and wanted us to fill out a Field Observation form to document our siting. She said that they were rare in the park and so they liked to document them when they sited them. I explained to her that we were amateurs and that we were not sure of its identity because our bird book said it didn't range there. She laughed and said, "If the book and the bird disagree, believe the bird."

Even as amateurs we can expand the reaches of research if we are accurate and detailed in our observations. My children have become very good at bird, insect, and plant identification because of their nature journals. Children are really very good at noticing details and love to make new discoveries. Math skills come in handy in the field. Noticing the time of day, weather conditions, location, distance, measurements, volume and length can all be important in documenting discoveries.

Another good exercise is to block off one square yard of ground and observe minutely the flora and fauna for one afternoon. Count the kinds of bugs and how many you see of each kind. What are they eating or doing? What about fauna that comes and goes? What plants are there? How many of each species? Describe the water, light and temperature. What is the soil like? Draw or describe everything carefully. Analyze your information. Make charts or graphs to help you understand what you have seen. How do you feel about that patch of earth after this experience? Look at it again after one month, or season by season. Record what you learn.

June 27, 1997

Common
Raven

21"

We saw three ravens at Weeping Rock each
time we passed. The large birds had low,
hoarse croaks. They seemed quite used to people
and apparently nest there every year.

Will spotted the Summer Tanager
in the cottonwoods near the river. Its
range in the guide was more southern.
We asked at the Nature
Center. They said they
are rare but do
range there. They
wanted us to fill out
a field observation form
saying we had seen
it. It was quite exciting.
It was a beautiful little
bird. Bright red in the sunlight
but nearly black in the shadows
of the tree limbs. They said,
"IF the bird and the book disagree,
believe the bird."

Summer
Tanager

♂
6½"

34

Cut-away pictures are fun too. Do a cut-away picture of a pond, showing the surface and under water views. Include animals, insects, and plants that occupy those habitats. Imagine the earth cut-away and how the roots and worms would look. Examine road cuts or cliffs and draw you observations. Think about the earth in different ways. The earth's journal is in her rocks.

Creating you own field guides for your neighborhood or town or state is fun. Start with the plants, birds, and animals that are most common in your habitat. When you are familiar with those things common to your area you will be more sensitive to rarer species as they occur. Having done this, trips become a great opportunity to see things not indigenous to your area. On trips my children like to list all the animals, plants or birds that we see along the way. They then choose one or more to paint and tell about. Often this leads further to study and research. We always ask lots of questions, the foundation of scientific inquiry.

1997 Date/Hour	Temp	suny or clouds	Rin or snow	Remarks Wind
Feb 25th 1:00 am	cold	(sun drawing)	no rain or snow	NW light / fun to play in.
feb 27 2:00	cold	(cloud drawing)	snow	NW light / fun To play in.
Mar 3 2:06 pm	4°C	c (cloud drawing)	snow	W / fun To play in
Mar 4	2°C	Clouds	snow	S / plax
mar 6 11:30	6°C	Suny (sun)	no rain or snow	SE / Warm
Mar 7 11:25	6°C 11.25	suny (sun)	no rain or snow	S / warm
mar 17 8:30	4°C 8:57	cloudy	rain	still / cold day
mar 19 12:00	20°	suny sqtact	no	S / warm
mar/23/98 1:54	55°C 1.89	suny and cloudy	no	N / very warm
4/13/98 2:28	390c 2.30	cloudy	rain	ive

Weather Chart

*When we try to pick out
anything by itself,
we find it hitched to
everything else in
the universe.*

— John Muir

Chapter 8

HISTORY AND GEOGRAPHY

History and geography have had the misfortune in the classroom of becoming dry, impersonal topics—dead topics, full of facts and names and numbers. A history or geography class fails when it has no foundation in the personal world of the student. If they can touch (physically if possible) the life of the student, they become adventures into the mysteries of the past. As in all areas of study, the challenge is not so much to know, but to care about the subject. You can make history personal through discovery journals.

In the family, go to sites that are personal in your child's own history. Where Dad proposed to Mom. Where Grandpa thought a rattlesnake bit him. Where Great-great-grandpa kept horses for the Pony Express when he was twelve. Take

time to imagine yourself back in that time. What things are the same and what has changed? Tell the story again on the actual site. Tell them in physical ways. "These are the stones they made the corral out of because there was no wood for a gate. William was twelve years old at the time and had to lift these stones away to get the horses out for the riders. Can you lift these stones?"

In Utah, Pioneer Day is a very popular holiday. It ranks right up there with Independence Day. On Pioneer day we sometimes spend the entire day outside doing pioneer things. We enjoy eating three meals outside, making butter, sewing quilt blocks for the girls, whittling for the boys, wearing sunbonnets and long sleeved shirts. We make a little log cabin (playhouse size) out of poles the boy scouts use for lashing. Grandma and Grandpa come and tell stories. We sing folk songs and wait for the stars to come out. We feel the hot July sun rise, simmer, and set. We are grateful for shade. No wonder the first settlers in this desert valley brought saplings from

This year we grew little four inch corn cobs of Indian corn. The children were quite happy with them when we popped it.

the canyons and watered them carefully with buckets of hauled water. Our sensations can help us imagine why things happened the way they did.

Historical re-enactment sites are wonderful adventures into history. Williamsburg in Virginia, Plymouth Plantation in New England, Wheeler Farm in Salt Lake City, a Renaissance Faire in San Bernardino, Shakespearian Festivals are wonderful. Go with the heart of a participant instead of a spectator. Wear costumes or an appropriate hat. This is living history. Try to feel a part of the festivities.

If you can't go to the actual site you can always pretend, and pretend with a flourish. One Thanksgiving we decided to go traditional with our turkey and corn. We carried the table and food outside, feasting in the frosty air. Keeping the food warm on our plates was hard. How cold was it in New England we wondered? Why did they feast for three days? How long does it take to cook a turkey on an open fire? Will there be enough food if thirty more friends drop in? How would Puritans act at a party? We learned to be thankful for central heating, electric stoves, hot and cold running water. We gave thanks for things of which the pilgrims never dreamed. They gave thanks for food and freedom, things we rarely appreciate. Personal, practical questions pumped life into our Thanksgiving lesson.

After these experiences you will have something to write about in your discovery journal. You will have personal feelings connected with the events. These discoveries will become a part of you in ways that memorizing dates for a Friday test never can.

I believe that history and geography make great friends. They support each other. History takes on new life when placed in a physical setting. Likewise, oceans and mountains and the rocks themselves, have shaped our histories as nations and individuals. The more we learn about natural history the more we understand our place in the world. Personal geographies tell us where we have been and where we hope to go.

Wheeler Historic Farm

Begin with the most personal setting you can remember. Do you have a secret place? Can you describe it? Paint it? What places have meaning to you? Remember the tree house your brother built, the place where you broke your arm, the corner of the yard you tried to make into a pond when you were nine. Go back to a former home and note how the trees have grown. What has changed over five years or twenty-five? Can you describe it so well that the next generation can find it twenty years hence? What changes and what lasts? Tell the story of the place in your journal. Put in history, setting, emotion, natural features, plants, streams, or cliffs. Tell how it has changed. Imagine how it may change. Our children love to drive by the house we moved from six years ago to check on the trees we planted. They are so tall now, the changes astound us.

Primarily, your journal should be personal— the things that make us care about a place. Places become part of us. They are the setting where we take root and grow, the place we run away from or the place we run away to. Sometimes the significance of these places take decades to reveal themselves. We may resolve them differently this year than we did last year or next. I was very rooted in my childhood home in San Diego— not the building, but the place. I wrote in my journal at seventeen:

> Every holiday we are able, my family goes tide pool hunting. We watch the sea creatures and collect shells and rocks. We all love the sea, moving, changing, living. Thanksgiving, Christmas, or New Year would not be the same to me without the ocean.

Now I have lived fifteen years in landlocked Utah, making a home for my children here— teaching them to love the mountains and deserts. Still, we go to California often. They all know my love for the ocean. Yet do they know how it feels in my soul? How it shapes who I am? I like to think it means more to them because of me. I want them to feel at home with the sea, knowing it is a part of me.

My grandmother was rooted in a place called Card Canyon, a side canyon of Logan Canyon in northern Utah. She had a cabin there. Her house was in town but her home was in the canyon. Every summer she would move her considerably large family (eleven children) to live in the canyon, escaping the summer heat of town. I see her in my memory, planted in her large rocker, surrounded by the sound of the river, all the windows (whole walls of them) open to the afternoon breeze and shimmering box elder trees. Always on the table sat a wildflower arrangement, sometimes fresh, sometimes dried. She loved the tiny flowers the best. My mother or dad would fry up rainbow trout caught from the river outside the door. Fish never tasted that good at home.

I remember Grandma camping with the family at reunions. Her sons would gently settle her in a camp chair in a shady spot of the group camping site. Wherever she was became the center of our activities. She is always eighty-three in my memories, with a large hat and a bowl of pine nuts next to her. We ran like the spokes on a wheel out to the boundaries our parents had set. We always came running back to her smile with grubby young hands full of flowers or pine cones or bugs. The uncles came back with fish stories and deer sightings. The aunts brought food and talked while they heated large pots of water on camp stoves for dishes and faces.

Now, when I walk in these Utah canyons I feel she walks with me. She saw the same wild flowers, wild birds, wild creatures that seem strange to me, having grown up on the coast. My father says she knew all their names. She is part of me, and she loved these things. I can love them too as I love her. How I would love to walk with her again and share her wild days.

Write your own natural history of your setting, your environment. The longer we live in a place the deeper the roots grow. Nevertheless, we are tough little plants. We survive transplanting, sometimes repeatedly. Some soils are more fertile, more acidic or alkali. Weather conditions change. Drought and blight effect us. Our settings make a difference. We spring from our history, nourished from its roots and sun and rain.

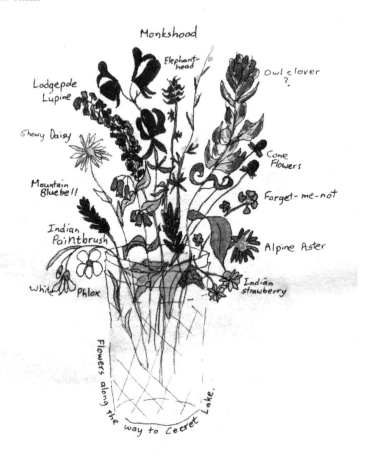

Monkshood
Elephant-head
Owl clover ?.
Lodgepole Lupine
Showy Daisy
Cone Flowers
Mountain Bluebell
Forget-me-not
Indian Paintbrush
Alpine Aster
White Phlox
Indian strawberry
Flowers along the way to Cecret Lake.

"Nature is God."

—Dante

Chapter 9

EXPANDING NATURE STUDIES
WITH HANDIWORK

One way to expand you nature studies beyond your journal activities is to explore nature crafts. Working with natural objects, turning them into useful or provocative expressions is fun for children and adults alike. Exploring the properties of your nature finds can increase respect and knowledge for the original. I find the most beautiful nature crafts preserve the beauty of the original creation. Nature crafts are popular because they give us the opportunity to feel our own creative sparks. They translate God's handiwork into very personal handiwork of our own. They spring from our desires to preserve and create.

My favorite nature crafts require few instructions, little expense, and the ability to see common objects in a new way. They change with the seasons, materials available, and my children's current interests. Here are a few ideas to get you started.

Bird bath. One year my children made a bird bath in the garden for Mother's day out of four large sticks (four feet long and two inches in diameter), a bit of rope, and the lid of a trash can. The birds loved it and so did I. Birds are attracted by any kind of water.

Bird feeders. There are many kinds of bird feeders. Our favorite is made from an empty two-liter pop bottle. Attach a coat hanger to the lid by poking a hole in the lid, pushing the wire through the hole and bending it over. Near the bottom, make holes so you can push two sticks, about a foot long each, completely through the bottle at right angles. This makes four perches for the birds to sit on. Two inches above each perch make a V-shaped hole about 3/4 of an inch high. Push the center of the V in slightly so the birds can reach the seed. Poke a few small holes in the very bottom to allow rain water to drain out. Fill the bottle with bird seed. Some feathered wanderer will discover it in a few days and invite his or her friends to the party.

Collecting. Seeds, rocks, shells, leaves, insects, photos, pine cones, abandoned nests, butterflies— anything can be the theme for a nature collection. Collections were a very popular pastime in the Victorian era. Now, we must be careful our collections are not going to harm nature's balance or disturb its beauty for another. The naturalist's rule of twenty should apply—don't remove it unless there is more than twenty like it nearby. We should not collect anything endangered or dangerous. We should not collect things without purpose. If, however, you do collect things, try to find a way to display your collections in an attractive or useful way. Soon you will lose the urge to collect things you already have. This is a great way to study the grand variety of nature. If you do come across a rare wild flower the best way to collect it and make it your own is by recording it in your discovery journal and leaving the blossom in the earth to fulfill its purpose for being. We would not dream of capturing a rare animal or bird for merely selfish reasons. Capture the memory instead, in your journal.

Cooking. Cooking can take on a new appeal when you know where the ingredients come from. This is especially good for children. Make some pies out of those Halloween pumpkins. Find an orchard where they will let you pick your own basket of fruit. Buy berries at a roadside stand and make them into jam or

syrup. We like to go to the farmers' market in the fall because the vegetables and fruits look so wonderful and sometimes you get a story about the food, as it were, straight from the farmer's mouth. I have not ventured much into wild foods— only things I am sure are safe like wild raspberries, asparagus, or mint. I would be sure to have a reliable guide and watch him eat it first. My suburb was once a farm so we can find wheat and barley in our empty lots and along the road side. How nice to know what the plants are, to teach our children where their daily bread comes from! One of my favorite children's stories is the Little Red Hen. She takes the wheat and plants it, tends it, harvests it, cleans it, grinds it into flour and bakes it into bread. Our children should experience this process. If everyone could experience the living education of making a loaf of bread from wheat harvest to spreading that pat of butter (homemade) onto the steaming slice, we might find ourselves one bite closer to heaven.

Corn husk dolls. Save your corn husks from your summer corn. Use them green or soak dried husks in water until flexible. Tie off the head with a bit of string, place the arms and tie the waist. Trim the skirt for girls or divide the legs and tie for boys. Experiment with some natural dies on the clothing parts. Boil onion skins for yellow. Spinach for green.

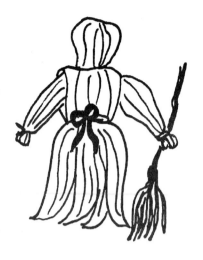

Beets for red. Walnut shells for nut brown. Place them in action poses to dry— like a mother sweeping with a twig broom or holding a baby. You can make little yarn dolls with this same design.

Daisy chains. I hope we all remember these. You make a tiny slit in the stem of the flower with your thumbnail and thread the next flower through the hole. Take that flower and do the same until your chain is long enough for necklaces or garlands.

Dandelion curls. Pick some dandelions with long stems. Puck off the blossoms. Split the stems and put them into a dish of water. The stems will curl into spirals. The thinner you split the stems the tighter the curls will be.

Dreams. Be sure to set aside plenty of time for dreams. With all our making and doing, creating and arranging, don't neglect the dreaming available in nature activities. Watch the clouds move, the wind in the trees, the light on the water, the sun on your back, the taste of the air. I have a penchant for staring out of windows as if in a trance. My husband has expressed a desire to know what I think about when I stare off into space like another world is visible. I don't know what to tell him. I am not thinking about anything in particular, not thinking at all would be closer to the truth. Just being. Letting my mind be empty, resting. I suppose I could call it meditation, or prayer. But it really isn't. It takes conscious thought to pray. Mental drifting is the closest I can come to describing it. Do it. Let your mind rest from lists and pictures and words, worries and joys, even dreams may be too concrete. Drift for a time with the clouds and the wind. Give yourself an empty place for the Holy Spirit to fill up. Allow your children to do it too. To dream. To be. To rest. Teach them to listen to their own meanderings.

Feathers. We have a shoe box full of feathers found on nature outings. Our pet birds also donate regularly. We like to try and remember the names of the birds they came from. Sometimes they make their way into pressed flower arrangements or decorate picture mats or presents. On a quiet day at home, they are fun to paint into our journals. Quill pens will give your writing a new flair.

Flower arranging. Fresh or dried, a flower arrangement adds grace to the table. I also like to use other interesting plants, cattails or small branches of maple leaves, or dried stalks that still hold on to their seed pods. Many times we bring home offerings from our walks for the table which we paint into our nature notebooks in the comfort of the kitchen. Here we can observe them at our leisure and often notice details that are lost in the field. Occasionally, the meal is interrupted by a science experiment or a dash for a reference book but such is life.

Flower pressing. It's easy to make a flower press with two squares of plywood and four screws with wing nuts. Cut layers of cardboard and paper the size of the plywood in which to place the flowers or leaves to be pressed. Be careful to choose flat, non textured paper or your flowers will have strange designs on them

not intended by nature. I have also had good success in our dry Utah climate with telephone books and large dictionaries. This did not work so well when I lived in San Diego. In

humid climates mold can be a problem. In that case, dry your findings more quickly in a food dehydrator or microwave. I inherited a large medical/cooking/veterinary book from my grandmother copyrighted in 1917. Among the herbal remedies I found some beautifully preserved specimens in the pages.

I try to collect and press flowers and leaves from my garden throughout the spring, summer, and fall. They pile up on a corner of my desk. I save them to examine on some dreary winter afternoon in January. At that time I sort out the successful pressings by type or size. I store them in plastic page protectors so I can turn quickly to the pansies or the ferns without disturbing them too much. Be sure to do a lot of ferns and leaves for backgrounds of the more showy flowers.

The possibilities for using pressed flowers really are endless. They can be used in papermaking, candles, stationary, or picture frames. Laminate them for bookmarks, report covers, identification booklets, window pictures, or place mats. They are lovely in framed art also. A watercolor with a few pressed flowers in the foreground  from the site of the painting gives a very personal touch to a landscape. Pressed flowers with handwritten scientific notes or a poem or pithy quote can inspire contemplation. Be sure to press some autumn leaves also. A handful of scattered autumn leaves makes a beautiful framed piece.

Gardening. Whether you use a window sill or a half acre, gardening can be an intimate way of exploring nature. Here you can watch the product from start to finish. Experience the effects of wind, rain, and frost. Watch growth and life cycles. Gardening is one of, if not the most, popular hobby in our country. In our affluence, most of us have been freed from the necessity of living off our crops and so can explore gardening in other realms. You can plant a vegetable garden, an herb garden, a butterfly garden, a flower garden, a medicinal garden, a privacy garden, a water garden, or a rock garden. The uses are endless. Experiment with new plant varieties, or several varieties at once to determine the best one for your soil and family. One year we tried purple beans. They were beautiful in the garden

and produced prolifically, but were not too popular on the table. According to the Bible, education began in a garden. Gardening will nourish the souls of young and old. Be sure to record your experiments and results in your nature journal so you will remember what you have tried from year to year.

Hiking sticks. My husband came into the marriage with a hiking stick. His staff had accompanied him on several John Muir Trail hikes through the Sierra Nevada mountains. It was polished smooth by his own sweaty hand. It had a name (Moses). He kept it by the front door of our apartment. Before long, he had found another thinner, shorter staff for me to polish on our hikes together. We gave it a name. He suggested that we measure them so that in fifty years we could tell how much wear the ends had endured. Needless to say, this family tradition has become cumbersome now that there are nine in our family. I argue that there are plenty of sticks along the trail if you need them, and after their service you can leave them in the forest. But, the children want to be like their daddy. And I want them to be. However, I have had to insist that the hiking sticks huddle together in the corner of the garage, now that we have a garage. Each of us knows his own. When the trail is steep or the river swift you want a thumb bump that fits your hand. So, look for a hiking stick you can make your own. Whittle off the bark, sand it smooth. Round off the top, preserve the knots that give it character and help your hand to feel at home. Give it a name. Carve your initials in the wood. Take it on long walks.

Leaf and bark rubbings or prints. This activity can awaken your senses to the textures of nature. Use regular blank paper and peeled crayons. Place the paper over the leaf on a flat surface. Fill the area with color and watch the shape of the leaf appear. For bark, wrap the paper around the trunk of the tree. You might enjoy doing a sample page for each type of tree in your neighborhood and sewing the pages together for a herbarium. Ink prints of leaves are also interesting. Use an inked stamp pad and a blotter of tissue or paper toweling as you press it on the page. Expand your palette by using water colors. Dip or soak dried leaves in a quarter cup of water with a drop or two of dish soap. This will soften the leaf and help the paint to stick. Then apply your colors directly to the leaf and press onto your paper. Inked prints will show the most detail. This is a fun winter project.

Natural clay. Try to find a strata of natural clay. I grew up on a mesa in San Diego that only had about two feet of top soil. My brother and I dug down into the layer of clay below that and found enough red clay to make tiny pots and a few bricks and other things that we dried in the sun like ancient natives. If that is not possible in your area, you can buy natural clay in big blocks at craft stores for a reasonable amount. You can let it dry to hardness and fire it if you choose. After my sixth baby was born a friend called to ask what she could bring over as a baby gift. Our church members often bring dinners or treats to new moms to simplify the first few days at home. I thanked her for her thoughtfulness but explained that we had already received enough food for a week. She pressed me further and I confessed that what I would really like was a block of clay to occupy the other children and let them know that they were important too. She laughed with understanding. She had six children of her own. She said it sounded easier than a casserole anyway. The children had a wonderful time creating things with the clay while I tended the baby and rested. It was a wonderful gift that I cherish in my heart.

Onion and garlic braids. When the onion and garlic is mature in the garden the tops dry out and fall over. Then it is time to dig up the aromatic bulbs for winter storage. I like to braid them together and hang them up to dry. Just brush the dirt off and start with the bulb end. Place the leaves into plaits. With every crossing leaf, place a new bulb in the strand. As you cross the next strand over the top it will fix the last bulb into place. Work your braid down a foot or two and tie it off with a bit of yarn. Hang it up to dry from the yarn end so the bulbs hang down. In January when I need an onion for the soup I just pluck one off the braid, peel it, and chop it unto the brew. They will last all winter if you plant enough.

Papermaking. Recycled newspapers, dryer fluff, or plant matter can be made into interesting papers for journal covers or art work. There are many ways of doing this so check out a few library books to get ideas. I've added water to the newspaper or fluff and blended it to a thin paste in my blender. Spread the paste on a horizontal window screen to dry. Squeeze out any extra moisture. Dried flower petals or grasses can be added at this point to the pulp. It may take a day or two to dry. Adding rice or wheat flour is interesting.

Photography. Nature photography can be very exacting. It helps if you have a powerful zoom lens and the conviction that one good picture in a roll is O.K.

Pine cones. Use for wreaths, Christmas tree decoration, package decoration, fire starters, centerpieces, smear with peanut butter and hang from a tree for the birds.

Potpourri. Collect your spent rose petals and other aromatic plants. Make sure they are dried thoroughly before storage. You can stuff sachets with the mix for your drawers.

Rock painting. You can paint on smooth rocks with acrylic paint to create menageries of interesting creatures, faces, symbols, etc.

Seed beads. Make necklaces or bracelets from different seeds or seed pods. You will need to soak the seeds first and have a strong needle and thread.

Stick pencils. Use a strong, straight, pencil-size stick, bark optional. Put it in a vise. Drill a straight hole through the center with a bit the size of your pencil lead. Put wood glue in the hole to fix the lead in place. Sharpen the end with a pocket knife.

Sun prints. This requires that you purchase light sensitive paper. It doesn't cost much and the results can be lovely enough for framing. I found my paper at an arboretum gift shop but I have seen it in home school catalogs and also science shops. You place a fern or flower on this special paper and expose it to the sun for a short time. The silhouette will appear on the paper.

Sundials. A straight stick and a paper plate will work for a day. Experiment with other materials.

Terrariums. Kids love to have their own little ecosystem to plant and tend. Its easy to see the water cycle, measure growth, and predict consequences. I'll never forget the terrarium my brother and I started in a gallon apple juice jar. After the school project was over, we tired of it and put it out in the garden under a large bush. Months later the original plants had died and the weeds had taken over. They were so robust that they broke the jar. What a lesson in letting weeds over take your garden!

Treasure Boxes. Let your children have a place for the things they bring home from their nature walks. The stone with a pretty color, the abandoned snake skin found on the trail, or the magpie's feather can be placed in a treasure box for safe keeping until they are painted into a journal, researched, placed in a collection or discarded for other treasures. Photo boxes make good treasure boxes. A sturdy shoe box could be decorated, painted or embellished with leaf prints to make a very personal treasure box. These treasures are fun to share with visiting relatives and friends.

Twigs. Twigs can be glued together to make interesting picture frames. They can be glued to make baskets for centerpieces or wastebaskets. They can be shaved into curls on one end for fire starting. It's fun to make a tiny log cabin out of real twigs.

Vegetable prints. Vegetable prints on paper bags make great wrapping paper. Dip the onions, apples, peppers, mushrooms, or whatever in tempera paint and press on the paper. You can carve potatoes and carrots into fanciful shapes if you choose. Stamp pads will work too.

Vines. Grapevines and spring willow branches can be woven into wreaths or baskets that stiffen as they dry.

Walking. Expand your nature studies by taking nature walks. It doesn't matter whether you walk in a nature preserve or around your city apartment building. Walking will improve your physical and emotional health. It will stimulate your intellect. It will increase your creativity. Notice the clouds, weather, wind, plants, birds, insects, pets, and how people and animals adapt to living together in your environment.

Wheat weaving. I am fortunate that I can find natural wheat along the roadside of my neighborhood. Glean the wheat when the heads are full but before they become wind-battered and lose their seeds. Cut the stems long. Soak it in hot water for a few hours to make the stems more pliable. Tie the heads together with a ribbon or raffia. Split the stems into two groups for braiding into the two sides of a heart. The seed heads hang down at the point of the heart. Shape the braids into a heart and tie the center dip together. When it is dry it will hold its shape. These look pretty on windows and doors. There are many other ways to twist and weave the stems.

Whistles. My favorite whistle is made from a long piece of field grass. You stretch it lengthwise between your thumbs while your thumbnails are both face up. Blow through the space between your thumbs which the blade of grass divides. You can modulate the tone by bending your thumbs.

Whittling. Many parents are afraid to let their children whittle for fear of accidents. Of course the child must have some level of maturity and an understanding of safety rules. Parents much judge when a child is ready for this age old activity. I associate very fond memories with my first pocket knife. As the youngest in the family it seemed I had to wait a long time to be allowed this privilege. When I was nine my father gave me a pocket knife for my birthday with the expected lessons on safety and sharpening. It was a coming-of-age present. I began by carving soap bars into rabbits. That summer I graduated to peeling the bark off of small sticks.

My joy was complete when we found we had forgotten our kitchen utensils for our camping trip to the Grand Canyon. For a week we cooked all our food on an iron griddle with wooden forks and stabbers whittled by my brother and me. Bacon and eggs never tasted so good.

Wind chimes. You can make these out of almost anything that will clank together. My favorites are made from shells (mussels work well) or metal tubing (lovely tones).

Chapter 10

DISCOVERING WILD PLACES

W here does one look for wilderness in today's world? Wilderness conjures images of exotic places somewhere else. But it can be very close. Wilderness edges into our lives at every turn, if we know where to look. Be observant, questioning, and open-minded.

A magnifying glass of some sort will help you to look at the world with new eyes. A child is a good companion for discovery. They experience the earth in physical imaginative

July 9th, 1997

Black-chinned Hummingbird 1.3"

♂

A slimmer body than the others. The purple throat looks black in all but the brightest of light

Broad-tailed Hummingbird ♂ L. 3½"
Only western hummer with solid red throat. Common in the Rockies. Ruby throated Hummingbird is the name of its eastern relative.

Rufous Hummingbird ♂ L. 3½"
Abundant migrant of the West. The rust coloring and the broad tail spread in flight distinguish it from the others.

ways. Imagine the world from above, like a bird, or below, like a cricket.

To study a tree, use your senses of touch, hearing, and smell. Look at it from above or beneath. Imagine the root system. Imagine it as a home for wild creatures. Look at the catkins of the spring, the colors of the autumn, the branching structure of winter trees, and the seed pods of summer.

In the home, you can do many things to bring a touch of nature to your life. You can grow interesting plants and herbs. Pets of all varieties are fun to draw while they sleep and play. Insects creeping in from the cold are interesting to study. You may enjoy sprouting grains of different sorts to observe their growth patterns. Window boxes bring nature almost inside. Wild bird feeders are simple to make and care for. They will bring wildlife to your window sill. When I am homebound, I can still enjoy watching the clouds through the window.

If you have the good fortune to have space for a little garden you can enjoy many hours of nature study. You don't need much space. A little spot with sun will do. My brother bought a home in California with a postage stamp of a yard, a patio, really. The previous owner had cemented it over. Still, he manages to grow quite a few vegetables by using container gardening. Use your garden to experiment with native plants, wild flowers, or unusual varieties. Jot down the seasonal changes, the blossoming times, the fruiting seasons in your journal. Make one month, one year and five year plans for your garden and sketch out those dreams in your journal.

Take walks in your neighborhood. Notice your neighbor's efforts to tame or welcome wilderness. Talk to your neighbors about their efforts. Especially look for older homes where the plantings are mature and time tested. Where has wilderness wedged her way back into your neighborhood through a crack in the sidewalk, a patch of weeds around a utility pole, an ant's nest, a pigeon's roost, or a rotting stump? You may be surprised by how much wilderness you find on your own city block.

If you venture forth on a short drive you can find city parks to contemplate, plant nurseries for research, road cuts for geology studies or empty lots to explore. Those empty lots are never really empty, you know. They are an oasis for weeds, insects, mice, birds, even wild flowers.

When you have the time for an afternoon outing, investigate nature centers, zoos, aviaries or botanical gardens. The farther you are willing to travel the more city parks you will find. Perhaps your city has set aside some natural green space. Where are the rivers and streams in your area? Are there other kinds of terrain, such as cliffs, canyons, beaches, mountains, or desert dunes? Is there a quarry? Where is the closest lake or pond? As much as we enjoy walking in the rain or snow, natural history museums can be a good alternative in bad weather.

Weekend trips are great adventures at our house. Although getting nine people and all their necessities in one vehicle takes some effort, it is worth it to get away from our everyday lives and discover new corners of the earth. We have visited historic sites, nature refuges, fish hatcheries, parks in other towns, forests, and highway turnouts. Rest stops often give us a chance to study a Joshua tree or sacred datura close up, notice the colors and temperatures of the soil, pick up a rock, or sight a bird that sends us scurrying back to the car for binoculars and field guides. If you have longer to spend, national parks are a must. We like to camp in the parks for several days at a time so we can leave the rushing behind and really enjoy the experience. The Junior Ranger programs are great for kids. Be sure to save time on your hikes to stop and paint, to dream and wonder.

I hope these suggestions will spark your interest in places near your home you have yet to investigate. We like to return again and again to favorite spots to enjoy the seasonal changes. Here are some places we return to regularly from our home base in Salt Lake City. They are in no particular order.

Utah's National Parks and Monuments: Zion's, Bryce Canyon, Arches, Dinosaur, Canyonlands, etc. (303) 969-2000 or visit their web site at www.nps.gov

Hansen Planetarium is a visit to the stars and planets from downtown Salt Lake City. (801) 538-2104 or visit the web at www.utah.edu/planetarium. The planetarium has a telephone number for astronomical events and star parties, (801) 532-STAR or (801) 532-7827.

Ogden Nature Center offers hands on exhibits with quiet walking trails. It is a 127 acre sanctuary with gardens designed to attract wildlife. Open 10 am to 4 pm, Monday through Saturday (801) 621-7595.

Red Butte Garden and Arboretum has stroller friendly trails which offer plenty of walking space. They label many rare plants for you. We like to visit every month to watch the changes in vegetation (801) 581-4747. Their web site is www.utah.edu/redbutte

Dimple Dell Regional Park is a 640-acre park along Dry Creek in southeastern Salt Lake County. It is three-and-a-half miles of wood chipped hiking trails. It is one of the few places left in the valley where one can see native plants and animals of the pre-settlement landscape. (801) 468-2299.

Hogle Zoo boasts the largest zoo in Utah. Their family pass has been a great investment. We go at least once a month, rain or shine. www.xmission.com/~hoglezoo/ or (801) 582-1631.

Jordan River Parkway Trail System is a pleasant urban trail along the banks of the Jordan River. Some sites of access to the trails are as follows:

• **Jordan River State Park** (Salt Lake City) runs from 200 North to 2200 North, 4.8 miles. (801)533-4496.

• **James Madison Park Trailhead** begins at 3300 South and the river to 3900 South through the Little Dell wetland's site. (801) 483-5473.

• **Redwood/Oxbow Area Trailhead** (Salt Lake County) begins at 100 West and 3100 South (access via 3300 South), leading over a bridge behind the County Oxbow Jail facility, and into a wildlife wetland complex. (801) 483-5473.

• **Arrowhead Park Trailhead** (Murray City) starts at 4800 South. It travels south to 6400 South. (801) 264-2614.

• **Winchester Park Trailhead** (Murray City) begins at 6400 South. (801) 264-2614.

• **Gardner Village Trailhead** (West Jordan City) has a fenced, paved trail on the north side of 7800 South at the historic Gardner Mill. It joins the Murray City trail. (801) 566-8903.

The **U.S. Forest Service** will provide information on many pretty spots in the area for hiking and camping. (801) 524-3908 or www.fs.fed.us

Tracy Aviary includes 7 acres of Liberty Park with more than one thousand birds. (801) 322-2473.

There are ten locations for **Utah State Fish Hatcheries** throughout the state. Group tours upon request. (801) 538-4717 or on the web at www.nr.utah.gov

This Is the Place Heritage Park is just north of Hogle Zoo. It is a living history park with pioneer farms and livestock. (801) 582-1847.

Wheeler Historic Farm is in the center of the valley. This may be your child's only chance to milk a cow by hand. (801) 264-2212.

Thanksgiving Point makes a relaxing afternoon outing. See goats, calves, sheep, llamas, ponies, buffalo, turkeys, rabbits, and ostriches. It is fun in the spring after the young ones arrive. It also has plants for sale, a tropical greenhouse, and cornfields. (801) 768-2300.

Little and Big Cottonwood Canyons are enjoyable drives in the early fall. Pull off the road and spend some time exploring. Bring your journal.

The **Temple Quarry** at the mouth of Little Cottonwood Canyon is a beautiful outing without much walking. You can see big horn sheep grazing on the mountainside. Bring binoculars.

The Spruces is a favorite campground in Big Cottonwood Canyon.

To find **Cecret Lake,** take the Little Cottonwood Canyon road to the very end (Albion campgrounds) and hike southwest 0.8 miles.

There is a **Beaver Dam** 1 mile up on an unmarked trail on the north side of Big Cottonwood Canyon.

Doughnut-hole Falls is a short 0.3 mile hike in Big Cottonwood Canyon.

Utah Museum of Natural History is found on the University of Utah campus (801) 581-6927.

The **Earth Science Museum** on the Brigham Young University campus displays Jurassic Period fossils. (801) 378-3680.

The **Monte L. Bean Museum** at Brigham Young University has displays of stuffed wildlife. It is free to the public. (801) 378-5051.

The kids love **Murray Park** with its large old trees, rose gardens, rivers, and trails.

Sugarhouse Park has a large city pond.

Timpanogos Cave is a few miles up American Fork Canyon. Plan on a good wait. They require tickets.

Alpine Loop Drive sparkles in the early summer while the wild flowers are in blossom. Head up American Fork Canyon and come down Provo Canyon, or vise-versa.

Cascade Springs nestles near the top of the Alpine Loop drive. Take the road that goes toward Heber. Cascade Springs is a massive crystal-clear spring with wildflower-lined trails. Look for the fallen log where we became engaged.

Don't miss the pioneer trail at **Big Mountain.** Take I-80 through Parley's Canyon, then take highway 65 until you get to the top of the pass. The trailhead is there. Heading east from Big Mountain gets you to Little Emigration Canyon, which is a gentle and quiet trail.

Ensign Peak has a great view of the valley. Head up from the State Capitol until you get to the highest paved street. From there hike up about one-half mile.

Grandma Faye's garden. The location of this one is our secret.

I am sure you will discover many more places, but these have been some of our family's favorites. Happy trails!

Appendix A
Books and videos with examples of Nature Notebooks

THE DIARY OF AN EDWARDIAN LADY
by Edith Holden. New York: Holt, Rinehart, and Winston, 1977.
— example of a nature notebook (mostly birds, leaves, poems, and folk lore)
— also a very fine video available through libraries of this book

THE SPRINGS OF JOY
by Tasha Tudor. New York. Simon & Schuster Books for Young Readers, 1998.
—beautiful thoughts and poems, beautifully illustrated

PAINTING NATURE IN PEN & INK WITH WATER-COLOR
by Claudia Nice. Cincinnati. North Light Books, 1998.
—full of step-by-step instructions on how to paint flowers, pebbles, birds, fish, reptiles, foliage, etc. Full of great watercolor tips

A TRAIL THROUGH LEAVES: A JOURNAL AS A PATH TO PLACE
by Hannah Hinchman. New York. W.W. Norton Company, 1997.
—a Valentine's day gift from my husband about journals and sketching

THE SIERRA CLUB GUIDE TO SKETCHING IN NATURE

by Cathy Johnson. San Francisco. Sierra Club Books, 1990.

—Excellent examples of nature sketch books and artistic advice. One of my favorites

DRAWING AND PAINTING FROM NATURE

by Cathy Johnson. New York: Design Press, 1989.

—written for the budding artist, lots of information on how to draw, keep a field sketchbook, use a camera, etc.

BEATRIX POTTER'S ART

by Anne Stevenson Hobbs. Penguin books, 1989.

— beautiful examples of childhood sketch books

— a peek into the Victorian naturalist and artist beyond her children's illustrations

CAPTURING NATURE: THE WRITINGS AND ART OF JOHN JAMES AUDUBON

by John James Audubon. New York. Walker, 1993.

—a book for young people with selections from Audubon's diaries

NATURE DRAWING—A TOOL FOR LEARNING

by Clare Walker Leslie. Englewood Cliffs, New Jersey: Prentice Hall, Inc. 1980.

—a classic, excellent examples of field work, prodigious illustrations, emphasis on learning rather than art itself although it includes suggestions on how to draw or render. The author has taught classes for all ages.

DRAWING FROM NATURE

by Jim Arnosky. New York: Lothrop, Lee and Shepard Books, 1982.

— Jim Arnosky has written several quickly read books full of lively pencil drawings that give insight into drawing in the field and taking notes. I have read several of these to my children. My children also loved his Crinkleroot series.

— *Secrets of a Wildlife Watcher*. New York: Beech Tree Books, 1991.

Great pictures and advice on how to sneak up on animals for observation.

— *Sketching Outdoors in Spring*. New York: Lothrop, Lee and Shepard Books, 1987.

NATURE'S SKETCHBOOK

by Marjolene Bastin. Look at Hallmark gift shops for her line of cards and notepapers.

Books by Louisa May Alcott and Gene Stratton Porter are consistent with Charlotte Mason's educational philosophies and keeping nature notebooks. While Charlotte Mason was educating her students in England, these American authors were sharing similar philosophies in their novels. They create an atmosphere in their books full of adventure and natural education.

Where *Little Women* may not appeal to all boys, try the books by Holling Clancy Holling. My boys loved these award winning books. *Paddle-to-the-Sea, Minn of the Mississippi, Seabird,* and *Tree in the Trail* will delight the whole family. These are books their Dad wanted to read to them. They are adventure stories full of history and imagination. The marginal notes and drawings remind me of journal sketches and enhance the text with facts.

Examples of Discovery Journals are also found in popular films. Check these to see others keeping notebooks.

DANCES WITH WOLVES,
BEATRIX POTTER'S ART
JUNGLE BOOK (Disney's live action), or
THE GIRL OF THE LIMBERLOST

Appendix B
Journals of Famous Men and Women

Many journals of notables have been published. Seek out the journals of your own heros. Many of these wrote and drew about their adventures in the wild. Many of them found inspiration for their life's work in nature. It is fascinating to read their journals and crawl right inside the minds of these great men and women. You can see into their souls. Here is a list to start with.

Teddy Roosevelt (politician, conservationist)

Aristotle (scientist, philosopher)

Lewis and Clark (explorers)

Beatrix Potter (children's author and illustrator)

Leonardo Da Vinci (scientist, artist, inventor)

John James Audubon (artist, naturalist)

Ernest Thompson Seton (co-founder of the Boy Scouts of America, artist, writer)

Charlotte Mason (educator of students and teachers)

Rachael Carson (biologist, writer)

Thomas Jefferson (farmer, politician, writer, musician)

John Muir (photographer, naturalist)

Louis Agassi (discovered Ice Ages)

Columbus (explorer)

Tasha Tudor (illustrator)

Thomas Alva Edison (inventor) *read about his camping trips*

Henry David Thoreau (writer, philosopher) *be sure to read his essay called "Walking"*

Roger Tory Peterson (ornithologist)

Emily Dickensen (poet)

Of course, you will think of others. I have been impressed by the diversity of gifts these men and women possessed. They used their journals to refine their many gifts and to move on to bless the world and those around them. I would that we may all do the same.

ABOUT THE AUTHOR

Karen Skidmore Rackliffe has been a pioneer and a leader in the rapidly growing home school movement since 1985. She is a founder of the Salt Lake Home Educator's Association and has been a leader in the Utah Home Education Association. She is a popular lecturer for these organizations and has spoken at several Charlotte Mason Conventions. Her articles on self-education have appeared in local, state and national newsletters and magazines. She has been a featured guest on talk radio and her home school was featured in *Utah Holiday Magazine* in July 1991. Her favorite lecture topic is nature journals.

She has a Bachelor's degree in Independent Studies from Brigham Young University. She has done extensive research on how children learn. She and her husband are the parents of seven children, who have been homeschooled with joy and success.